DIAGNOSIS
OF OUR TIME

A

INTERNATIONAL LIBRARY OF SOCIOLOGY
AND SOCIAL RECONSTRUCTION

Editor : Dr. Karl Mannheim

DIAGNOSIS OF OUR TIME

Wartime Essays of a Sociologist

by

KARL MANNHEIM

No Wind makes for him that hath no
intended port to sail unto.

MONTAIGNE

KEGAN PAUL, TRENCH, TRUBNER & CO., LTD.
BROADWAY HOUSE, 68–74 CARTER LANE
LONDON, E.C.

First published in England January 1943
Second Impression September 1943
Third Impression May 1945
Fourth Impression June 1947

THIS BOOK IS PRODUCED IN COMPLETE
CONFORMITY WITH THE AUTHORIZED
ECONOMY STANDARDS

Printed in Great Britain
by T. and A. Constable Ltd., Hopetoun Street,
Printers to the University of Edinburgh

CONTENTS

Part II. Christian Values and the Changing Environment

PREFACE

WITH the exception of one (Chapter V), these essays were written in war-time. They originated as lectures or as memoranda for groups who wanted to know what the sociologist had to say about certain aspects of the present situation.

For a while I hesitated to publish them in their original shape, and in normal times perhaps I should have preferred to knit them together more closely. But it was felt that the direct approach and the personal appeal should not be sacrificed to a more systematic and academic treatment. The independent essay, which can be read for itself and can become the basis of group discussion, conveys more directly the essential ideas than a comprehensive treatise. The book, as it stands, attempts to apply the method and the accumulated knowledge of scientific sociology to our reality. By shelving the work for later elaboration the time might be missed for whatever small contribution it might make to the discussion of the burning issues of the moment.

There are constellations in history in which certain possibilities have their chance, and if these are missed the opportunity may well be gone for ever. Just as the revolutionary waits for his hour, the reformer whose concern it is to remould society by peaceful means must seize his passing chance. For years it has been my conviction, which I have tried to bring home in my lectures and other activities, that Britain has the chance and the mission to develop a new pattern of society, and that it is necessary that we should become aware of it and act on it. In various ramifications this idea is applied in the present book to some concrete problems of the day.

It remains to indicate some of the occasions when the papers were read:

I. "Diagnosis of our Time": January 1941, lecture at a Conference of Federal Union at Oxford; July 1941, at the Week-End Summer Meeting of the Delegacy for Extra-Mural Studies, University of Oxford, Oxford; August 1941, at the International Gathering of Friends Service Council at Woodbrooke.

II. "The Crisis in Valuation": January 1942, lecture in a series of public lectures on "The War and the Future" given by various speakers and arranged by the London School of Economics (University of London) at Cambridge.

III. "The Problem of Youth in Modern Society": April 1941, opening address to the New Education Fellowship Conference at Oxford; May 1941, lecture given to the Masaryk Society, Oxford; July 1941, at Youth Leaders' Conference at Oxford, arranged by the Board of Education.

IV. "Education, Sociology and the Problem of Social Awareness": lecture at the University of Nottingham jointly arranged by the Institute of Education (University of London), Goldsmith College (University of London) and Nottingham University; lecture given to a group of members of the staff of the University of Newcastle, Durham, both in May 1941.

V. "Mass Education and Group Analysis": reprint from *Educating for Democracy*, planned and edited by J. I. Cohen and R. M. W. Travers. Macmillan, London, 1939.

VI. "Nazi Group Strategy": B.B.C. Overseas broadcast, 1941; reprint from *The Listener*, 19th June 1941.

VII. "Towards a New Social Philosophy": see footnote, p. 100.

Acknowledgments and thanks are due for permission to reprint to Messrs. Macmillan and Co., and to the British Broadcasting Corporation.

I wish to express special thanks to the Social Research Division of the London School of Economics (University of London) for a grant for a scientific research assistant. In this capacity Dr. Charlotte Luetkens collected documentary material which forms a part of the background of these studies; she helped me in editing the manuscript and I owe much stimulation to the discussions I have had with her. I also take this opportunity to thank all those who in discussion groups or after the lectures contributed to a broader understanding of the problems.

I

DIAGNOSIS OF OUR TIME

I. The Significance of the New Social Techniques

Let us take the attitude of a doctor who tries to give a scientific diagnosis of the illness from which we all suffer. There is no doubt that our society has been taken ill. What is the disease, and what could be its cure? If I had to summarize the situation in a single sentence I would say: "We are living in an age of transition from laissez-faire[1] to a planned society. The planned society that will come may take one of two shapes: it will be ruled either by a minority in terms of a dictatorship or by a new form of government which, in spite of its increased power, will still be democratically controlled."

If that diagnosis be true, we are all in the same boat—Germany, Russia, Italy, as well as Britain, France and U.S.A. Although in very many respects still different, we are all moving in the same direction towards a kind of planned society, and the question is whether it will be a good sort of planning or a bad one; for planning with dictatorship or on the basis of democratic control will emerge. But a diagnosis is not a prophecy. The value of a diagnosis does not mainly consist in the forecast as such, but in the reasons one is able to give for one's statements. The value of a diagnosis consists in the acuteness of the analysis of the factors which seem to determine the course of events. The main changes we are witnessing to-day can ultimately be traced to the fact that we are living in a Mass Society. Government of the masses cannot be carried on without a series of inventions and improvements in the field of economic, political and social techniques. By "Social Techniques"[2] I understand the sum of those methods which aim at influencing human behaviour and which, when in the hands of the Government, act as an especially powerful means of social control.

Now the main point about these improved social techniques is not only that they are highly efficient, but that this very same efficiency fosters minority rule. To begin with, a new military technique allows a much greater concentration of power in the hands of the few than did the technique of any previous period. Whereas the armies of the eighteenth and nineteenth centuries were equipped with rifles and guns, our armies work with bombs, aeroplanes, gas and mechanized units. A man with a rifle threatens only a few people, but a man with a bomb can threaten a thousand. That means that in our age the change in military technique contributes a great deal to the chances of a minority rule.

The same concentration has occurred in the field of government and administration. Telephone, telegraph, wireless, railways, motor-cars and, last but not least, the scientific management of any large-scale organization—all these facilitate centralized government and control. Similar concentration can also be observed in the means of forming public opinion. The mechanized mass production of ideas through press and wireless works in this direction. Add to this the possibility of controlling schools and the whole range of education from a single centre, and you will realize that the recent change from democratic government to totalitarian systems is due here also not so much to the changing ideas of men as to changes in social technique.

The new science of Human Behaviour brings into the service of the Government a knowledge of the human mind which can either be exploited in the direction of greater efficiency or made into an instrument playing on mass emotions. The development of the social services, especially of social work, allows the exertion of an influence which penetrates into our private lives. Thus, there is a possibility of subjecting to public control psychological processes which formerly were considered as purely personal.

The reason why I lay such emphasis on these social techniques is that they limit the direction in which modern society can develop at all. The nature of these social techniques is even more fundamental to society than the economic structure or the social stratification of a given order. By their aid one can hamper or remould the working of the economic system, destroy social classes and set others in their place.

I call them techniques because, like all techniques, they are neither good nor bad in themselves. Everything depends on the use that is made of them by the human will. The most important thing about these modern techniques is that they tend to foster centralization and, therefore, minority rule and dictatorship. Where you have bombs, aeroplanes and a mechanized army at your disposal, telephone, telegraph and wireless as means of communication, large-scale industrial technique and a hierarchic bureaucratic machinery to produce and distribute commodities and manage human affairs, the main decisions can be taken from key positions. The gradual establishment of key positions in modern society has made planning not only possible but inevitable. Processes and events are no longer the outcome of natural interplay between small self-contained units. No longer do individuals and their small enterprises arrive at an equilibrium through competition and mutual adjustment. In the various branches of social and economic life there are huge combines, complex social units, which are too rigid to reorganize themselves on their own account and so must be governed from the centre.

The greater efficiency, in many respects, of the totalitarian states is not merely due, as people usually think, to their more efficient and more blatant propaganda, but also to their instant realization that mass society cannot be governed by techniques of the homespun order, which were suited to an age of craftsmanship. The terror of their efficiency consists in the fact that by co-ordinating all these means they enslave the greater part of the population and superimpose creeds, beliefs and behaviour which do not correspond to the real nature of the citizen.

In this description of the concentration of social techniques I consciously refer to changes which characterize the very structure of modern society. That means, if the main reason for what happened in Germany, Italy, Russia and the other totalitarian countries is to be sought in the changed nature of social techniques, it is only a question of time and opportunity when some group in the so far democratic countries will make use of them. In this connection a catastrophe like war, rapid depression, great inflation, growing unemployment, which make extraordinary measures necessary (i.e. concentration of the maximum power in the hands of some Government), is bound to precipitate this process. Even before the outbreak of the war the present tension brought about by the existing totalitarian states forced the democratic countries to take measures very often similar to those which came into force in the totalitarian countries through revolution. It goes without saying that the tendencies towards concentration must greatly increase in a war when conscription and the co-ordination of food and other supplies becomes necessary.

After this brief description of the social techniques you might rightly say: "What a gloomy prospect. Is there a remedy for this? Are we simply the victims of a process which is blind but stronger than all of us?" No diagnosis is complete unless it seeks for a kind of therapy. It is only worth studying the nature of society as it is, if we are able to hint at those steps which, taken in time, could make society into what it should be. Fortunately, a further attempt at a diagnosis reveals to us some aspects of the situation which not only free us from the feeling of frustration but definitely call upon us to act.

II. THE THIRD WAY: A MILITANT DEMOCRACY

What I have so far described are social techniques. Like all techniques, they are neither good nor bad in themselves. Everything depends on the use that is made of them by human will and intelligence. If they are left to themselves and develop unguarded they lead to dictatorship. If they are made to serve a good purpose and are continually checked, if they do not master men but are mastered by men, they are among the most magnificent achievements of mankind. But we shall be able to turn the flow of events and avert the fate of Germany, Italy and Russia only if we are vigilant and use our knowledge and judgment for the better. The principle of laissez-faire will not help us any further, we shall have to face the forthcoming events at the level of conscious thought in terms of concrete knowledge of society. Such an analysis will have to start with some preliminary clarifications which might help us in defining our policy.

First of all—not all planning is evil. We shall have to make a distinction between planning for conformity and planning for freedom and variety. In both cases co-ordination plays a great rôle, co-ordination of the means of social techniques such as education, propaganda, administration, etc.; but there is a difference between co-ordination in the spirit of monotony and co-ordination in the spirit of variety. The conductor of an orchestra co-ordinates the different instruments and it rests with him to direct this co-ordination to the achievement of monotony or of variety. The goose-step co-ordination of the dictators is the most primitive misinterpretation of the meaning of co-ordination. Real co-ordination in the social sphere means only a greater economy and a more purposeful use of the social techniques at our disposal. The more we think about the best forms of planning, the more we might arrive at the decision that in the most important spheres of life one should deliberately refrain from interference, and that the scope for spontaneity should rather be kept free than distorted by superfluous management. You might plan the time-table of a boarding-school and come to the decision that at certain hours the pupils should be left entirely free—it is still planning if you are the master of the whole situation and decide that with certain fields of life one should not interfere. This sort of deliberate refraining from interference by a planner will radically differ from the purposeless non-interference of the laissez-faire society. Although it seems obvious that planning should not necessarily mean goose-step co-ordination, it was the bureaucratic and militaristic spirit of the totalitarian states which distorted the meaning of planning in that way.

There is a simple reason why in the long run great society cannot survive if it only fosters conformity. The French sociologist Durkheim first pointed out in *The Division of Labour in Society* [3] that only very simple societies like those of primitive peoples can work on the basis of homogeneity and conformity. The more complex the social division of labour becomes, the more it demands the differentiation of types. The integration and unity of great society is not achieved through uniform behaviour but through the mutual complementing of functions. In a highly industrialized society people keep together because the farmer needs the industrial worker, the scientist, the educationist, and vice versa. Besides this vocational differentiation, individual differentiation is needed for the sake of inventions and efficient control of the new developments. All this only corroborates our statement that the bureaucratic and military ideal of planning must be replaced by the new ideal of the planning for freedom.

Another necessary clarification is that planning need not be based upon dictatorship. Co-ordination and planning can be done on the basis of democratic advice. There is nothing to prevent parliamentary machinery from carrying out the necessary control in planned society.

But it is not only the abstract principle of democracy which must be saved as well as recast in a new form. The increasing demand for social justice has to be met if we wish to guarantee the working of the new social order. The working of the present economic system, if left to itself, tends in the shortest possible time to increase the differences in income and wealth between the various classes to such an extent that this itself is bound to create dissatisfaction and continuous social tension. But as the working of democracy is essentially based upon democratic consent, the principle of social justice is not only a question of ethics but also a precondition of the functioning of the democratic system itself. The claim for greater justice does not necessarily mean a mechanical concept of equality. Reasonable differences in income and in the accumulation of wealth to create the necessary stimulus to achievement might be maintained as long as they do not interfere with the main trends in planning and do not grow to such an extent as to prevent co-operation between the different classes.

This move towards greater justice has the advantage that it can be achieved by the existing means of reform—through taxation, control of investment, through public works and the radical extension of social services; it does not call for revolutionary interference, which would lead at once to dictatorship. The transformation brought about through reform instead of revolution also has the advantage that it can reckon with the help of former leading democratic groups. If a new system starts with the destruction of the older leading groups in society, it destroys all the traditional values of European culture as well. Ruthless attacks on the Liberal and Conservative intelligentsia and the persecution of the Churches are designed to annihilate the last remnants of Christianity and humanism and to frustrate all efforts to bring peace to the world. If the new society is to last, and if it is to be worthy of the efforts humanity has made so far, the new leadership must be blended with the old. Together they can help to rejuvenate the valuable elements in tradition, continuing them in the spirit of creative evolution.

But it is obvious that a new social order cannot be brought about simply by a more skilful and human handling of the new social techniques—it needs the guidance by the spirit, which is more than a system of decision on technical issues. The system of laissez-faire Liberalism could leave the final decisions to chance, to the miracle of the self-equilibrating forces of economic and social life. The age of Liberalism, therefore, was character- ized by a pluralism of aims and values and a neutral attitude towards the main issues of life.

Laissez-faire Liberalism mistook neutrality for tolerance. Yet, neither democratic tolerance nor scientific objectivity means that we should refrain from taking a stand for what we believe to be true or that we should avoid the discussion of the final values and objectives in life. The meaning of tolerance is that every- body should have a fair chance to present his case, but not that nobody should ardently believe in his cause. This attitude of neutrality in our modern democracy went so far that we ceased to believe, out of mere fairness, in our own objectives; we no longer thought that peaceful adjustment is desirable, that freedom has to be saved and democratic control has to be maintained.

Our democracy has to become militant if it is to survive. Of course, there is a fundamental difference between the fighting spirit of the dictators on the one hand, who aim at imposing a total system of values and a strait-jacket social organization upon their citizens, and a militant democracy on the other, which becomes militant only in the defence of the agreed right pro- cedure of social change and those basic virtues and values—such as brotherly love, mutual help, decency, social justice, freedom, respect for the person, etc.—which are the basis of the peaceful functioning of a social order. The new militant democracy will therefore develop a new attitude to values. It will differ from the relativist laissez-faire of the previous age, as it will have the courage to agree on some basic values which are acceptable to everybody who shares the traditions of Western civilization.

The challenge of the Nazi system more than anything else made us aware of the fact that the democracies have a set of basic values in common, which are inherited from classical antiquity, and even more from Christianity, and that it is not too difficult to state them and to agree on them. But militant democracy will accept from Liberalism the belief that in a highly differentiated modern society—apart from those basic values on which demo- cratic agreement will be necessary—it is better to leave the more complicated values open to creed, individual choice or free experimentation. The synthesis of these two principles will be reflected in our educational system in so far as the agreed basic virtues will be brought home to the child with all the educational methods at our disposal. But the more complex issues will be left open to save us from the evil effects of fanaticism.

The main problems of our time can be expressed in the following questions. Is there a possibility of planning which is based upon co-ordination and yet leaves scope for freedom? Can the new form of planning deliberately refrain from interfering except in cases where free adjustment has led not to harmony but to conflict and chaos? Is there a form of planning which moves in the direction of social justice, gradually eliminating the increasing disproportion in income and wealth in the various strata of the nation? Is there a possibility of transforming our neutral democracy into a militant one? Can we transform our attitudes to valuations so that democratic agreement on certain basic issues becomes possible, while the more complex issues are left to individual choice?

III. THE STRATEGIC SITUATION

Our diagnosis would be incomplete if we examined the possibilities in the abstract only. Any sociological or political therapy must devote special attention to the concrete situation in which we find ourselves. What is then the strategic situation? There are a number of forces which seem to be moving automatically in the direction which I have indicated above. First, there is a growing disappointment with laissez-faire methods. It is gradually being realized that they have been destructive, not only in the economic field where they produced the trade cycle and devastating mass unemployment, but that they are partly responsible for the lack of preparedness in the liberal and democratic states. The principle of letting things slide cannot compete with the efficiency of co-ordination—it is too slow, is based too much upon improvization and encourages all the waste inherent in departmentalization. Secondly, there is a growing disappointment about Fascism for, although it seems to be efficient, its efficiency is that of the devil. Thirdly, there are grave doubts concerning Communism, even in the minds of those to whom—as a doctrine—it first meant the panacea for all the evils of Capitalism. Not only are they forced to ponder upon the chances of Communism if it were to be introduced by revolutionary methods into the Western countries with their differentiated social structure, but they cannot close their eyes to certain changes which took place in the time between Lenin and Stalin. The more they have to admit that what has happened was an inevitable compromise with realities, the more they have to take into account the presence of these realities also elsewhere. What these realities teach us is, briefly, that Communism works, that it is efficient and has great achievements to its credit as far as the state of the masses goes. The miscalculation begins with the fact that neither Dictatorship nor the State seems to wither away. Marx and Lenin believed that dictatorship was only a transient stage, which would disappear after the establishment of a new society. To-day we know that this was a typical nineteenth-century delusion. When Marx conceived this idea, one could point to the fate of absolutism which everywhere was slowly giving way to democracy. But this process, in the light of our analysis, was due to the fact that in the nineteenth century social techniques were still very inefficient and those in power had to compromise with the forces working from below. In a modern totalitarian state once the whole apparatus is appropriated by a single party and its bureaucracy, there is little chance that they will give it up of their own accord.

Thus there is at least a chance that out of the general fear and disillusionment a more reformist attitude may develop. War automatically created a united front—a kind of natural consensus which is needed for such reform. Ultimately it depends on us whether we can take full advantage of this unanimity. The question of the moment is whether we understand the deeper meaning of the so-called Emergency Measures. These are a step towards the necessary co-ordination of the social techniques at our disposal without giving up democratic control based upon the co-operation of all parties. Of course, many of these emergency measures cannot, and should not, remain permanent. But some of them must endure, as they are simply an expression of the basic fact that the vital needs of the community should everywhere and always override the privileges of individuals. On the other hand, if we are to preserve the great traditions of Western civilization, we must vigorously defend those rights of the individual upon which real freedom depends. In this struggle for a new and stronger authority combined with new forms of freedom we must base our selection upon conscious principles in the building up of a new system.

To this analysis of the strategical situation one may object that the political unity engendered by the war cannot be expected to last, once the threat of the common enemy is removed. The advantage of a war emergency from the standpoint of planning is that it creates a unity of purpose. My answer to this is that, whatever the outcome of this war may be, the menace of social and economic chaos will be imminent and may replace the threat of Fascist aggression. Of course this threat will only produce co-operation between groups and parties if under the pressure of the situation they are capable of creative adjustment, if they are capable of a type of response which is on a higher level of morality and based upon a fuller understanding of the situation than is required under normal conditions. If this happens there could well be co-operation and agreement upon certain basic, long-range issues, and the transition to a higher stage of civilization could be planned. As in the life of the individual, so in the life of nations, the hour of crisis reveals the presence of fundamental vitality. We must prepare the ground now for a full realization of the significance of the hour.

The unbridled criticism of the form of freedom and democracy which has existed in the past decades must therefore cease. Even if we agree that freedom and democracy are necessarily incomplete as long as social opportunities are hampered by economic inequality, it is irresponsible not to realize what a great achievement they represent and that through them we can enlarge the scope of social progress. Progressive groups will be readier to advocate reformist measures, as it is becoming obvious that recent revolutions tend to result in Fascism and that the chances of a revolution will be very slight as soon as a united party has co-ordinated all the key positions and is capable of preventing any organized resistance.

The depressing experiences of the past few years have taught us that a dictatorship can govern against the will of even a large majority of the population. The reason is that the techniques of revolution lag far behind the techniques of government. Barricades, the symbols of revolution, are relics of an age when they were built up against cavalry. This means that there is a high premium on evolutionary methods. As to the ruling classes, there is a chance that the more intelligent sections within them may, under changed conditions, prefer a gradual transition from the present unplanned stage of Capitalism to a democratically planned society with social aims to the alternative of Fascism. Although Fascism does not formally deprive them of their property, State interference is growing and will ultimately subjugate them. The strategical problem in their case consists in splitting their ranks in such a way that the would-be Fascists among them are severed from those who have only to lose in a Fascist experiment.

In my opinion, a new social order can be developed and the dictatorial tendencies of modern social techniques can be checked if our generation has the courage, imagination and will to master them and guide them in the right direction. This must be done immediately, while the techniques are still flexible and have not been monopolized by any single group. It rests with us to avoid the mistakes of former democracies, which, owing to their ignorance of these main trends, could not prevent the rise of dictatorship, and it is the historical mission of this country on the basis of her long-standing tradition of democracy, liberty and spontaneous reform to create a society which will work in the spirit of the new ideal: "Planning for Freedom."

II

THE CRISIS IN VALUATION

I. Conflicting Philosophies of Life

At first only a few people were aware of the approaching chaos and the crisis in our system of valuations. They noticed that the religious and moral unity which integrated mediaeval society was vanishing. Still, the disintegration was not yet quite apparent, because the Philosophy of Enlightenment seemed to offer a new approach to life with a unified purpose, out of which developed the secularized systems of Liberalism and Socialism. No sooner had we made up our mind that the future would resolve itself into a struggle for supremacy between these two points of view than a new system of valuation emerged, that of universal Fascism. The basic attitude of the new outlook is so different from that of the previous systems that their internal differences seem almost to vanish.

Thus, in the very same social environment we now have the most contradictory philosophies of life. First, there is the religion of love and universal brotherhood, mainly inspired by Christian tradition, as a measuring-rod for our activities. Then there is the philosophy of Enlightenment and Liberalism, with its emphasis on freedom and personality, and its appreciation of wealth, security, happiness, tolerance and philanthropy as the means of achieving them. Then we have the challenge of the Socialists, who rate equality, social justice, basic security and a planned social order as the chief desiderata of the age. But beyond all this we have, as I said before, the most recent philosophy, with the demoniac image of man emphasizing fertility, race, power, and the tribal and military virtues of conquest, discipline and blind obedience.

We are not only divided against each other in our evaluation of the big issues, such as the principles of the Good Life and those of the best social organization, but we have no settled views, especially in our democratic societies, concerning the right patterns of human behaviour and conduct. One set of educational influences is preparing the new generation to practise and defend their rational self-interest in a competitive world, while another lays the emphasis on unselfishness, social service and subordination to common ends. One set of social influences is guided by the ideal of asceticism and repression, the other by the wish to encourage self-expression.

We have no accepted theory and practice concerning the nature of freedom and discipline. Some think that, owing to the self-regulating powers inherent in group life, discipline would spontaneously emerge if only full freedom were given and the pressure of external authority removed. In contrast to this anarchist theory, others hold that if strict regulation is applied to those spheres of life where it is necessary, the scope for real freedom is not suppressed but rather created. To such thinkers discipline is the pre-condition of freedom. Having no settled views on freedom and discipline, it is not surprising that we have no clear-cut criteria for the treatment of criminals, and do not know whether punishment should be retributive and deterrent or a kind of readjustment and re-education for life in society. We hesitate whether to treat the law-breaker as a sinner or as a patient, and cannot decide whether he or society is at fault.

But the crisis in valuations does not only come to the fore in marginal cases of maladjustment such as crime; we have no agreed educational policy for our normal citizens, since the further we progress the less we know what we are educating for. On the primary levels of education we are undecided whether to aim at creating millions of rationalists who discard custom and tradition and judge each case on its merits, or whether the chief aim of education should be the handing on of that social and national inheritance which is focussed in religion. On the higher levels of education we do not know whether to educate for specialization, which is urgently needed in an industrialized society with a strict division of labour, or whether we should cater for all-round personalities with a philosophical background.

Again, it is not only in the world of education that we are hazy; we are equally vague concerning the meaning and value of work and leisure. The system of working primarily for profit and monetary reward is in process of disintegration. The masses are craving for a stable standard of living, but over and above that, they want to feel that they are useful and important members of the community, with a right to understand the meaning of their work and of the society in which they live. While this awakening is going on amongst the masses, there is a split in the ranks of the wealthy and educated few. To some their high position and accumulated wealth means primarily the enjoyment of limitless power; to others, an opportunity for applying their knowledge or skill, giving guidance, shouldering responsibility. The first group represent the potential leaders of Fascism, the latter are those who are willing to assist in building up a new social order under competent leadership.

As I have said it is not only work but also leisure that is subjected to entirely different interpretations and valuations. The puritan sense of guilt in connection with leisure and recreation is still at war with the emerging hedonistic cult of vitality and health. The idea of privacy and contemplation, and of their value, is at war with that of mass enjoyment and mass ecstasy. The same division of opinion appears in regard to our sex habits. Some still condemn sex altogether, trying to place it under a taboo, while others see a remedy for most of our psychological maladjustments in the removal of mystery and repression from that sphere of life. Our concepts and ideals of femininity and masculinity vary according to the different groups, and the lack of agreement creates conflicts which permeate not only philosophical discussions but also the day-to-day relations of men and women.

Thus there is nothing in our lives, not even on the level of basic habits such as food, manners, behaviour, about which our views are not at variance. We do not even agree as to whether this great variety of opinions is good or bad, whether the greater conformity of the past or the modern emphasis on choice is to be preferred.

There is, however, one last issue about which we are clear. It is definitely not good to live in a society whose norms are unsettled and develop in an unsteady way. We realize this even more now that we are at war, when we must act quickly and without hesitation and fight an enemy whose value system is deliberately simplified in order to achieve quick decisions. In peace-time it might have been stimulating for the historian and the individual thinker to study the great variety of possible responses to the same stimulus and the prevailing struggle between different standards and differences in outlook. But, even in peace-time, this variety in valuations tended to become unbearable, especially in marginal situations where a simple "yes" or "no" was required. In such situations, many a man faced with the slowness of democracies in making their decisions came to share the view of a well-known Fascist political scientist who said that a bad decision is better than no decision. This is true to the extent that the indecision of the laissez-faire system represents a drifting which automatically prepares the ground for the coming dictator. Thus, long before the outbreak of war a few far-sighted thinkers became aware of the dangers inherent in the crisis in valuations, and tried to find the deeper causes of that crisis.

II. CONTROVERSY ABOUT THE CAUSES OF OUR SPIRITUAL CRISIS

The two chief antagonists in the controversy about the causes of our spiritual crisis are the Idealists and the Marxists. To religious thinkers and philosophical idealists it seemed clear from the outset that the crisis in valuations was not the effect but rather the cause of the crisis of our civilization. To them all the struggles of history were due to the clash between different forms of allegiance to authority or to changing valuations. The abandonment of Christian and then of humanitarian valuations by modern man is the final cause of our crisis, and unless we restore spiritual unity our civilization is bound to perish. To the Marxist the exact opposite is true. What is happening in the world at present is nothing but a transition from one economic system to another and the crisis in values is, as it were, the noise made by the clash of these systems.

If you are a Liberal, your advice is to free the economic order from State interference with markets and let things of the spirit take care of themselves. If you are a Marxist, you see ideologies and valuations as a part of the social process, but in your strategy you too often focus your attack alone upon the economic aspects of society and hope that after the establishment of the right economic order a world of harmony will automatically emerge by the very action of dialectical interdependence. As the source of all our discord is to be sought in the antagonisms inherent in the Capitalist system, it is only natural that its removal will put everything right.

I think it was the great merit of the Marxist approach, as compared with the purely idealistic one, that it realized once for all that the life of culture and the sphere of valuations within it depend on the existence of certain social conditions, among which the nature of the economic order and of the corresponding class structure is of primary importance. This opened up a field of investigation which we call the sociology of culture. On the other hand, the exclusive emphasis on the economic foundations limited from the outset the outlook of the emerging sociology of culture. In my view, there are many other social factors and conditions upon which the life of culture depends, and the vocabulary of a sociology which approaches the crisis of culture with categories of "class" only is far too limited, as is the view that economic and class factors alone are responsible for the crisis in our valuations.

The difference in outlook will become explicit when we consider the remedy which follows from the two sociological approaches, the Marxist and that which I am to expound. According to the Marxist, you have only to put your economic house in order and the present chaos in valuation will disappear. In my view, no remedy of the chaos is possible without a sound economic order, but this is by no means enough, as there are a great many other social conditions which influence the process of value creation and dissemination, each of which has to be considered on its own merits.

In my sociological approach, as in the Marxist's, it is futile to discuss values in the abstract; their study must be linked up with the social process. To us values [1] express themselves first in terms of choices made by individuals: by preferring this to that I evaluate things. But values do not only exist in the sub-jective setting as choices made by individuals; they occur also as objective norms, i.e. as advice: do this rather than that. In that case they are mostly set up by society to serve as traffic lights in the regulation of human behaviour and conduct. The main function of these objective norms is to make the members of a society act and behave in a way which somehow fits into the pattern of an existing order. Owing to this dual origin, valua-tions are partly the expression of subjective strivings, partly the fulfilment of objective social functions. Thus there is a con-tinuous adjustment at work between what individuals would like to do if their choices were directed by their personal wishes only, and what society wants them to do.

As long as the structure of society is simple and static, established valuations will last for a very long time, but if society changes this will immediately be reflected in the changing valuations. Re-valuations and re-definitions of the situation will necessarily accompany the changed structure of society. A new social order cannot exist without these re-valuations and re-definitions, as it is through them alone that individuals will act in a new way and respond to new stimuli. Thus the valuation process is not simply an epiphenomenon superstructure, an addition to the economic order, but an aspect of social change in all its provinces where changed behaviour is wanted. But if valuations in their most important functions act as social controls, like traffic lights, it is obvious that we cannot bring order and harmony into the chaos of these controls unless we know a little more of the social processes which make these controls work, and about those social conditions which may upset the working of that signal system.

There is definitely a coherent system of social and psychological activities which constitute the process of valuation; among them value creation, value dissemination, value reconciliation, value standardization, value assimilation are the most important, and there are definite social conditions which favour or upset the smooth working of the process of valuation.

And this is exactly my contention. There has been a complete displacement of the social factors on which the smooth working of the process of valuation depended. But we have been so society-blind that we could not even properly distinguish these factors, let alone put right what went wrong. What I am going to do, therefore, is to try to enumerate some of those changed social conditions which upset the traditional functioning of the main factors in the process of valuations.

III. Some Sociological Factors upsetting the Process of Valuation in Modern Society

(1) The first set of disturbances in the sphere of valuations arises from the simple fact of the uncontrolled and rapid growth of society. We pass from a stage where the so-called primary groups, family, neighbourhood, form the background to one where the larger contact groups prevail. As C. H. Cooley [2] has pointed out, there is a corresponding transition from primary attitudes and virtues to derivative group ideals. The primary

virtues of love, mutual help, brotherhood are deeply emotional and personal, and it is quite impossible to apply them without adjustment to the setting of larger contact groups. It is possible to love your neighbour whom you know personally, but it is an impossible demand to love people of a wider area whom you do not even know. In Cooley's view it is the paradox of Christianity that it tried to apply the virtues of a society based upon neighbourly relationships to the world at large. It did not only ask you to love the members of your tribe (a demand by no means peculiar to Christianity), but also to love the whole of mankind. The solution to the paradox is that the commandment "Love your neighbour" should not be taken literally but should be translated according to the conditions of a great society. This consists in setting up institutions embodying some abstract principle which corresponds to the primary virtue of sympathy and brotherliness. The equal political rights of citizens in a democracy are abstract equivalents of the concrete primary virtues of sympathy and brotherliness.

In this case it is the method of translation which makes the value system function once more. But only social workers could tell us how often people fail in life because they never have been taught how to translate the virtues in which they have been trained in their homes into the conditions of society at large. To educate for family life and neighbourhood functions is different from educating for national and world citizenship. Our whole educational tradition and value system is still adapted to the needs of a parochial world, and yet we wonder that people fail when they are expected to act on a broader plane.

(2) Whereas in this case the method of translation helped to give meaning to primary virtues in a world of widening contacts, in other cases values of the neighbourly world will only function adequately under modern conditions if they are linked up with complete reform. Take, for example, the whole system of valuations which is linked up with the idea of private property. This was a creative and just device in a society of small peasants or small independent craftsmen, for, as Professor Tawney[3] has pointed out, in this case the law of property only meant the protection of the tools of the man who did socially useful work. The meaning of the norm completely changes in a world of large-scale industrial techniques. Here the very same principle of the

private ownership of the means of production implies the right to the exploitation of the many by the few.

This example shows from another aspect how, through the transition from simpler conditions to more complex ones, the very same rule, i.e. that of private property, may change its meaning completely, and may grow from an instrument of social justice into one of oppression.   It is not enough to give a conscious reinterpretation of the value system organized around the idea of property; a complete reform is needed if the original intention, that the value of social justice should prevail, is to be put into practice again.

(3) The transition from a pre-industrial world where handicrafts and agriculture prevailed is not only reflected in the changing meaning of the valuations, which are focussed in the property concept, but also in a changing set of aesthetic valuations and of values regulating our habits of work and leisure.   It would not be at all difficult to demonstrate how in our appreciation of art the real struggle lies between the attitudes which are rooted in good craftsmanship and values which emanate from machine-made goods.

But the antagonism of values exists even more conspicuously in valuations which are linked up with the labour process.   The working incentives and rewards of the pre-industrial age are different from those of our age.   The prestige of the various occupations in a society of hand-made goods is different from the forms of prestige which emerge in the hierarchy of the factory and the business organization.   New forms of individual and collective responsibility emerge, but very often the lack of opportunity for taking responsibility depresses those who still strive for self-respect through the skill invested in their work. It has rightly been said that our society has not yet assimilated the machine.   We have successfully developed a new type of "taylorized" efficiency which makes man part of the mechanical process and moulds his habits in the interests of the machine. But we have not yet succeeded in creating those human conditions and social relationships in the factory which would satisfy the value aspirations of modern man and contribute to the formation of his personality.

The same applies to our machine-made leisure.   The wireless, the gramophone and the cinema are now tools for producing and distributing new patterns of leisure. They are democratic in nature and bring new stimuli into the life of the humblest, but few of them have yet developed those genuine values which would humanize and spiritualize the time spent outside the workshop, factory and office.

Thus the machine age has either been incapable of producing adequate new values which would shape the process of work and leisure, or else is incapable of reconciling two different sets of competing ideals, both of which in their antagonism tend to disintegrate human character instead of integrating it. The same effect is visible in most of modern man's activities, as whatever he does in one compartment of his life remains unrelated to the others.

(4) Confusion in the sphere of valuation arises not only out of the transition from the conditions of the past to those of the present, but also through the growing number of contacts between groups. Through the growth in the means of communication and through social mobility such as migration or the rise and fall in the social scale, values of different areas are dropped into the same melting-pot. Formerly one could refer to different value areas: habits, customs and valuations of one county differed from those of another, or the scale of valuations in the members of the aristocracy differed from that of the burghers. If groups made contact or even fused, there was time for assimilating one another's values; a kind of incorporation took place, and differences did not remain unreconciled nor survive as antagonistic stimuli. To-day we embody the most heterogeneous influences in our value system, and there is no technique for mediation between antagonistic valuations nor time for real assimilation. Against this background it becomes clear that in the past there were slow and unconscious processes at work, which carried out the most important functions of value mediation, value assimilation and value standardization. These processes are now either displaced or find neither time nor opportunity to do their work properly. This in itself reduces the value experience to insignificance. If a dynamic society is to work at all it needs a variety of responses to the changing environment, but if the variety of accepted patterns becomes too great it leads to nervous irritation, uncertainty and fear. It becomes gradually more and more difficult for the individual to live in a shapeless society in which

even in the simplest situations he has to choose between various patterns of action and valuations without sanction; and he has never been taught how to choose or to stand on his own feet.

To counteract the ill-effects of this variety one would have to find some method of a gradual standardization of basic valuations in order to regain balanced attitudes and judgments. As this is lacking in our mass society, it is to be feared that out of the uncertainty there will emerge the cry for dictated values.

(5) Another source of displacement and disturbance in our value system is due to the entirely new forms of authority and sanctions which have emerged, and to the new methods of justifying existing authority and sanctions. When society was more homogeneous the religious and political authorities coincided at many points, or else there was a violent conflict to define the spheres of the religious and political authorities. But now we are faced with a variety of religious denominations and the disagreement between various political philosophies which, as all of them act at the same time, only succeed in neutralizing each other's influence upon the minds of the people.

Added to this we have the different methods of justifying authority. At one time there were only two ways of justifying the authority of social regulations: either they were a part of tradition ("as our forefathers have done it") or they expressed the will of God. Against this, the new method of value justification grew up, which acknowledged as its one source of acceptance that which could be deduced from eternal rational law, supposedly common to the human race. When this belief in enlightenment by the Universal Ratio as lawgiving power disintegrated, the door was thrown open to value justification of the most various kinds. The Utilitarian justification of values by their usefulness or the belief in the uncontrollable inspiration of the Leader became as plausible as the belief in the law of the strongest. Whether the latter finds expression in the theory of an eternal struggle between races, classes or élites is not of primary importance. In all these cases there is no end to the process of mutual extinction, as the justification is such as to admit endless arbitrary claims: why should not my leader have the vision, my race or class the vocation, to rule the world?

Another difficulty of the same order is that of focussing responsibility on some visible social agent. Where there is no

B

acknowledged value system authority is dispersed, methods of justification become arbitrary and nobody is responsible. The focussing of authority and the allotment of different grades of responsibility to different functionaries are pre-conditions of the functioning of social life. But this focussing becomes more difficult as different classes, with their varying historical origins and mental make-up, adhere to different standards and as no attempt is made to reconcile their differences.

(6) An even worse predicament of our age is caused by the fact that whereas the most important values governing a society based upon the rule of custom were blindly accepted, the creation of the specifically new values and their acceptance is to a large extent based upon conscious and rational value appreciation. Whether one should love one's neighbour and hate one's enemy is based, as we have seen, upon the belief that this is either a demand of God or a part of our ancient traditions, but whether the democratic organization is preferable to the dictatorial one, or whether our educational system should pay more attention to the study of classics or to further specialization, these are decisions which have to be argued. Even if we agree that finally the preference might rest upon some irrational decision, persuasion has to go through the stage of conscious deliberation, and new techniques of conscious value appreciation are continually in the making.

Although this process leading to greater consciousness and deliberation is in itself a great advance, yet when it is brought into the existing social context it completely upsets the balance between conscious and unconscious forces operating in our society. The change to conscious value appreciation and accept-ance is a Copernicus-like change on the social plane and in man's history, and it can only lead to improvements if it is really assimilated by society at large. To bear the burden of a greater amount of consciousness is only possible if many other things (among them education) are changed at the same time. The origins of this upsetting novelty are to be found in those days when man for the first time realized that through the conscious direction of law he could somehow influence a changing society. He thereby realized that it was possible to link up value creation and value guidance with conscious deliberation, to foresee and to some extent influence social effects. What is happening now is that what is already a matter of course in the legal sphere is being transferred to other spheres. In the spheres of education, pastoral work and social work, values of a moral rather than a legal nature are being linked up with rational deliberation and appreciation. Thus value creation, value dissemination, value acceptance and assimilation become more and more the concern of the conscious ego.

(7) This change is formidable, as in order to create a law-abiding citizen whose obedience is not solely based upon blind acceptance and habit, we ought to re-educate the whole man. People who are conditioned to accept values blindly either through obedience, imitation or emotional suggestion will hardly be able to cope with those values that appeal to reason and whose underlying principles can and must be argued. We have hardly realized yet, to its full extent, what a tremendous reform of education would be necessary to make a democratic society, based upon conscious value appreciation, function. There is one thing every reformer and educationist ought to bear in mind, and that is, that every new system of social controls requires the re-education of the self. In a society where the value controls were traffic lights directly appealing either to conditioned responses or to the emotions and the unconscious mind, one could bring about social action without strengthening the intellectual powers of the ego. But in a society in which the main changes are to be brought about through collective deliberation, and in which re-valuations should be based upon intellectual insight and consent, a completely new system of education would be necessary, one which would focus its main energies on the development of our intellectual powers and bring about a frame of mind which can bear the burden of scepticism and which does not panic when many of the thought habits are doomed to vanish.

On the other hand, if our present-day democracy comes to the conclusion that this frame of mind is undesirable, or that it is impracticable or not yet feasible where great masses are concerned, we ought to have the courage to build this fact into our educational strategy. In this case we ought, in certain spheres, to admit and foster those values which appeal directly to the emotions and irrational powers in man, and at the same time to concentrate our efforts on education for rational insight where

this is already within our reach. It is possible to follow both
courses: to train completely for irrational values in a society
which is based upon them, or to train for rational deliberation
where the values are such as to allow a great deal of rational
justification on utilitarian grounds, for instance. But what is
destined to lead to chaos is a clash between the nature of predominant valuations and the existing methods of education. You
cannot create a new moral world mainly based upon rational value
appreciation, i.e. values whose social and psychological function
is intelligible, and at the same time maintain an educational
system which in its essential techniques works through the
creation of inhibitions and tries to prevent the growth of judgment. The solution seems to me to lie in a kind of gradualism
in education, which acknowledges stages of training where both
the irrational approach and the rational find their proper place.
There was something of that vision in the planned system of the
Catholic Church, which tried to present the truth to the simple
man through images and the dramatic processes of ritual, and
invited the educated to face the very same truth on the level of
theological argument. There is no need to emphasize the fact
that my reference to the Catholic Church is not to be interpreted
as a recommendation of her dogma, but as an example showing
how educational policy might be planned in a way that takes
into account different types of value reception.

(8) We have seen some of the social causes making for crisis in
our laissez-faire societies. We have seen how the transition from
primary groups to great society, the transition from handicrafts
to large-scale industrial techniques, the contacts between formerly
separated value areas, caused disturbances in the process of
valuation. We have seen how the new forms of authority and
sanctions, the new methods of justifying authority, the lack in
the focussing of responsibility and the failure to educate for
conscious value appreciation, each by itself and all of them
together contribute to the present crisis in valuations. We have
finally seen how all the mechanisms which used to regulate
automatically the process of valuation have gradually been
weakened or eliminated without being replaced by anything else.
It is no wonder, therefore, that our society lacks that healthy background of commonly accepted values and everything that lends
spiritual consistency to a social system. If there is any truth in

the Aristotelian statement that political stability depends on the adaptation of education to the form of government, if at least we agree with those who realize that a society can only function when there is a certain harmony of prevailing valuations, institutions and education,—then our laissez-faire system is bound sooner or later to disintegrate.

In a society where disintegration has proceeded too far, the paradoxical situation arises that education, social work and propaganda, notwithstanding highly improved techniques, become less and less efficient because all the values that could guide them tend to evaporate. What is the use of developing exceedingly skilful methods of propaganda and suggestion, new techniques of learning and habit-making, of conditioning, de-conditioning and re-conditioning, if we do not know what they are for? What is the good of developing child guidance, psychiatric social work and psychotherapy if the one who is to guide is left without standards? Sooner or later everyone becomes neurotic, as it gradually becomes impossible to make a reasonable choice in the chaos of competing and unreconciled valuations. Only those who have seen the result of complete non-interference with valuations and deliberate avoidance of any discussion of common aims in our neutralized democracies, such as Republican Germany, will understand that this absolute neglect leads to drifting and prepares the ground for submission and dictatorship. Nobody can expect a human being to live in complete uncertainty and with unlimited choice. Neither the human body nor the human mind can bear endless variety. There must be a sphere where basic conformity and continuity prevail.

Of course, if we complain that our liberal and democratic system is left without a focus, we certainly do not want a regimented culture and an authoritarian education in the spirit of the totalitarian systems. But there must be something, a third way, between totalitarian regimentation on the one hand and the complete disintegration of the value system at the stage of laissez-faire on the other. The third way is what I call the democratic pattern of planning or planning for freedom. It consists essentially in the reverse of a dictatorial imposition of external controls. Its method is either to find new ways to free the genuine and spontaneous social controls from the disintegrating effects of mass society, or else to invent new techniques which perform the function of democratic self-regulation on a higher plane of awareness and purposeful organization.

By now it must have become obvious why I dwelt so long on the analysis of the main changes that have effected the working of the various factors in the process of valuations. One will also understand why I tried to enumerate some of the remedies, the techniques of readjustment in the process of valuations as, for instance, translation of values, creation of new values, complete reform, value assimilation, value standardization, value reconciliation, focussing of authority and responsibility, training in conscious value appreciation, etc. As the democratic planning of the value system will not consist in the inculcation of values, the careful study of the factors which make the spontaneous value process work in all its aspects in everyday life becomes an urgent task.

If we agree that real planning is democratic planning, then it follows that the problem is not whether we should plan or no, but to find the real difference between dictatorial and democratic planning. The development of the method of democratic value guidance, as it is gradually being worked out in the Anglo-Saxon democracies, and which, I hope, will be worked out even more in the future, is outside my scope here. I can only state some of the principles by which such a democratic form of value policy could be guided.

IV. The Meaning of Democratic Planning in the Sphere of Valuations

(1) The first step to be taken by the democracies in contrast to their previous laissez-faire policy will consist in giving up their complete disinterest in valuations. We must not shrink from taking a clear stand when it comes to valuations, nor maintain that in a democracy agreement on values is not feasible.

Since the outbreak of war, and even more recently, since the main enemy became universal Fascism, the predominant fronts have changed and new opportunities for consensus have emerged. The question is mainly, whether we rightly understand the meaning of that change and are ready to act on it promptly.

The very fact that the democracies are fighting their war against Fascism, a war which will have to continue on a spiritual plane even when the actual fighting is over, has made it imperative to emphasize both the unifying elements in our democratic system and a progressive evolution of the social implication of democracy. That means that there is an inherent tendency in the present situation to bring to the fore the appreciation of the values of the democratic way of life and of democracy as a political system and not to discard them for any promise of a better world. On the other hand, I think the situation contains sufficient pressure not to allow the need for consensus to become a screen behind which we could remain socially stagnant or even reactionary. This would mean losing the war and the peace. Of course, this chance for achieving consensus and social progress is only a chance. To make it real calls for a great deal of awareness and courage.

(2) The second desideratum to make a democratic value policy feasible is to bring home to every citizen the fact that democracy can only function if democratic self-discipline is strong enough to make people agree on concrete issues for the sake of common action, even if they differ on details. But this self-restraint will only be produced on the parliamentary scene if the same virtues are being exercised in everyday life. We know that the parliamentary machinery can only produce the necessary consensus and compromise if the very same processes of value adjustment are continually at work in everyday life. Only if in daily contacts the habit of discussion produces reconciliation of antagonistic valuations and the habit of co-operation produces mutual assimilation of each other's values can it be hoped that a common policy can be hammered out in parliament, where the big organized parties meet and have to define their aims and strategy.

It is, of course, not enough to state this as a general desideratum. It wants a whole campaign to find out which are the sore spots in the social fabric where social disease, institutional deterioration and dehumanization set in. Consensus is far more than theoretical agreement on certain issues—consensus is common life. To prepare the ground for consensus eventually means to prepare the ground for common life.

Reformers have occasionally brought the evils of a social system into the limelight of common knowledge and concerted action: what these men have achieved occasionally, will now have to be done on a large scale and systematically. It is hardly

possible to assume in an age like the present one that the detrimental effects of, e.g., unemployment, malnutrition or lack of
education remain confined to certain classes of society. The strict
interdependence of events in modern society makes the general
unrest, which goes with physical and mental destitution, the
concern of all. To prepare the ground for consensus ultimately
means to remove these environmental obstacles. The struggle
for common valuations, therefore, is bound to go hand-in-hand
with the struggle for social justice.

Yet, on the other hand, one cannot assume that greater social
justice will automatically produce agreement on a basic set of
valuations. In mass society there are many other sources of
disagreement and individual and group antagonisms which lead
to chaos if they are not properly dealt with. It will be one of the
principal tasks of the sociologist to study the conditions under
which disagreement arises and where the process of group adjustment and value reconciliation fails to function in the context of
everyday life. He will analyse the causes of failure with the same
empirical methods of investigation which in so many other fields
pointed out remedies for institutional deterioration.

It is one of the achievements of modern sociology that it
discovered empirically remedies for social evils which formerly
were simply looked upon as the result of ill-will and sin. If
sociology was able to assist in defining the social causes of various
types of juvenile delinquency, the roots of gang behaviour, the
processes which make for race-hatred and other forms of group
conflicts, it is only natural to assume that it will be possible to
suggest methods which might assist people in their daily adjustments and mediate in their disagreements on valuations.

If a society were to invest as much energy, e.g., in the mitigation of race and group hatred as the totalitarian societies in their
fostering of it, important achievements in the mitigation of
conflicts could be achieved. Conciliation committees and courts
of arbitration present a pattern of spontaneous agreement on
issues on which others would wait for a command. As an example of what arbitration combined with sociological knowledge can do, one of the most remarkable documents is the
Chicago Commission's Report on Negro Riots.[4] After the outbreak of these riots a committee was set up in order that it might
use its sociological knowledge to discover the causes, both great

and small, which were responsible for the disturbances. Even if one realizes the limitations of the report, it provides some indication of how collective maladjustments and valuation differences could one day be treated if we found new kinds of institutions to deal with them adequately and on an appropriate scale.

(3) But the task of a democratic value policy is not only to mitigate conflicts and maladjustments after they have become apparent; it has also positively to care for the growth of that basic agreement. If the sociological statement is true that no society can survive without co-ordination of basic valuations, institutions and education, there must be democratic ways of fostering the growth of such a harmony in great society. Education, adult education, social work, juvenile courts, child guidance clinics, parent education represent some of the institutions, old and new, which are instruments in our hands. But the existence of these means of value dissemination, value adjustment and value assimilation is not enough. What is needed is a more conscious philosophy of their meaning, a more deliberate co-ordination of their policy and a focussing of their efforts on the strategically important points. This focussing of effort in our democratic world need by no means lead to a dictatorship, for, apart from the fact that this policy would be democratically agreed, there would still be scope for experiment and freedom for minorities to have their own ways.

The main point in all these suggestions is that democracy does not necessarily mean a shapeless society, a society without a value policy but one in which spontaneous integration of consensus on different levels continually takes place. Denominational groups, local groups, interest groups, professional groups, age groups will develop a variety of approaches to valuations, but it is essential to supplement the divergence by a machinery of co-ordination and value mediation which culminates in a collectively agreed value policy, without which no society can survive.

It is wrong to think that these integrating efforts are necessarily superimposed on natural group life, whereas the disintegrating forces, i.e. individual and group selfishness, are genuine. Both tendencies are equally at work in every living society and even in each individual. The trouble about mass society is that the social mechanisms which ought to guide value integration and mediation are being continually suppressed.

One of the lessons we can learn from the war is how many psychological and institutional forces can become operative in a society, if integration is really wanted. We ought to observe these mechanisms carefully, as the future of society depends upon whether we can devise a technique for coming to an agreement about basic valuations and the methods of social reform. Otherwise the only alternative is dictatorial planning. In this context there is much truth in the statement of the psychologist William James that the problem of modern society is to find a moral substitute for war. That means, to find a unifying purpose which acts as strongly as war in stimulating a spirit of altruism and self-sacrifice on a large scale, but without an actual enemy.

I think there is a reasonable chance at least that after the horrors of this war the tasks of reconstruction will be so urgent that they will be felt by many to be a unifying issue at least as strong as the war itself. The dangers involved in failing to achieve a democratic reorganization of the world might act as a pressure similar to that of the fear of the enemy. If that fear is coupled with and led by intelligence, the problem of democratic planning could be solved. If this does not happen, the enslavement of mankind by some totalitarian or dictatorial system of planning will follow, and once it is established it is hard to see how it could ever be removed, or wither away by itself. Only with a profound sense of the magnitude of the issue can the problem of democratic planning and its value aspects be solved.

III

THE PROBLEM OF YOUTH IN MODERN SOCIETY

The problem of Youth in modern society has two aspects which can be formulated in the following two questions: What can Youth give us? and What can Youth expect from us?

Here I shall try to answer the first question only: What is the meaning of Youth in society? What can Youth contribute to the life of society?

The framing of the questions shows sufficiently that the sociological approach to the problem of Youth is new in two respects. The sociologist no longer thinks of education and teaching as a super-temporal method only, but is very much concerned with the concrete nature of society, in which Youth finds itself and to which Youth will have to make its contribution. There are, of course, some elements in the psychology and in the sociology of education which are general, but the picture is only complete if the general approach is supplemented by the analysis of the historical background and concrete context for which, and in which, Youth has to act.

The other innovation of the sociological approach is that it thinks of Youth and Society in terms of complete reciprocity. That means that the answer to the question what Youth ought to be taught and how it ought to be taught depends to a large extent on the nature of the contribution to society one expects Youth to make. By becoming society-conscious we no longer formulate the needs of Youth in the abstract, but always with reference to the needs and purposes of a given society. Our modern educational movements of the last decades, healthy as they were in realizing for the first time the rights of Youth and its genuine needs, were still limited and one-sided in that they over-emphasized the claims of Youth without paying due attention to the needs and claims of society. The modern educational movement with its experimental schools often behaved like wealthy parents towards their children. By asking themselves exclusively how to make the life of the child easy and how to provide him with everything and at all costs, they pamper the

31

child and reduce in him the potentialities of adjusting himself to adverse situations. "The Century of the Child" believed that every period of life was self-sufficient and had its own exclusive rights, and thus disregarded the equally important forces making for reciprocity between age-groups and society.

Whereas the old authoritarian education was blind to the vital and psychological needs of the child, the laissez-faire of Liberalism disturbed the healthy balance of individual and society by focussing its attention almost exclusively on the individual and neglecting the concrete environment of society at large to which the individual is expected to make his contribution.

I. The Sociological Function of Youth in Society

The first problem that strikes us is this: Is the significance of Youth in society always the same? Obviously not. There are societies where the older people enjoy far greater prestige than the younger, who carry little weight as, e.g., in ancient China. There are other societies where, as in the U.S.A., after forty a man is very often deemed too old for a job and only the young people matter. But it is not only as to prestige of the young people that societies differ, but also as to whether the young are integrated into groups or into a movement which, as such, influences the course of events. Before the last war, in Germany a spontaneous Youth movement sprang up, which was neither supported by, nor even in favour with, the official groups and institutions ruling the country. England then experienced no such self-organization of her Youth, whereas France had a somewhat similar movement on a much smaller scale.[1] Russia, Nazi Germany, Fascist Italy and Japan to-day have state-organized, monopolistic organizations of Youth with a decidedly militaristic element.[2] England and other democratic states have nothing which corresponds to this. The sociological problem is that, although there always arise new generations in terms of younger age-groups, it depends on the nature of a given society whether it makes use of them, and it depends on the sociological structure of that very same society how it makes use of them. Youth belongs to those latent resources which every society has at its disposal and on the mobilization of which its vitality depends. There was never a better opportunity for realizing the truth of this statement than in the present war-time situation, when the survival of countries depends on the mobilization of their latent resources. Victory depends on the absorption of the last unemployed, on the use made of women in industry and on the use made of capital. But victory depends equally on the full use made of that psychological reserve which exists in the human mind or in the nation; on the mobilization of the capacity for sacrifice, courage, endurance and initiative. In this respect the analogy of the social body with the human body can be carried very far. Physiologists tell us that any given organ of the body normally works at one-eighth of its capacity and thus has seven-eighths in reserve. Under so-called normal conditions these reserves remain latent, but if a sudden crisis occurs or a reorganization of the basic attitudes is needed, the survival of the body will depend on the capacity of a quick and right mobilization of these resources.

It is not very difficult to guess which are those societies in which the prestige is with the old and in which the revitalizing forces of Youth do not integrate into a movement but remain only a latent reserve. I believe that static societies which develop only gradually, and in which the rate of change is relatively low, will rely mainly on the experience of the old. They will be reluctant to encourage the new potentialities latent in the young. Their education will be focussed on the transfer of tradition, their methods of teaching will be reproductive and repetitive. The vital and spiritual reserves of Youth will be deliberately neglected, as there is no will to break with the existing tendencies in society.

In contrast to these static or slowly changing societies, the dynamic societies which want to make a new start, whatever their social or political philosophy may be, will rely mainly upon the co-operation of Youth. They will organize their vital resources and will use them in breaking down the established direction of social development. In this respect there are differences of degree only between societies which bring about change through revolution or reform. In both cases, as long as there is a will to make a new start, it will have to be done through Youth. The older or intermediate generations may be able to foresee the nature of the forthcoming changes, their creative imagination may be used to formulate new policies, but the new life will only be lived by the younger generations. They will live the new values which the older profess in theory only. If this is true, the specific function of Youth is that it is a revitalizing agent; it is a kind of reserve which only comes to the fore if such a revitalization is wanted for adjustment to quickly changing or completely new circumstances.

The mobilization of this vital reserve is again in many ways similar to that in the body. According to modern biologists, the most important physiological process is that action should be transformed into function. For example, the baby shows a great number of random movements which in themselves mean nothing but a sheer expression of vitality. Growth, experience, training and education consist in transforming these haphazard movements into functional activities through processes of integration and co-ordination. The same applies to society. Many activities are latent in society which remain unused. Feeling, emotion and thought become socially significant only if they are integrated. Let me give an example to illustrate this. All of us know that the greatest oppression in history is not that of the slaves, serfs or wage-earning labourers, but that of women in patriarchal societies. And yet the sufferings and the resentment of these women remained meaningless throughout the many thousand years as long as they were sufferings of the millions of individual women in isolation. But their resentment at once became creative and socially relevant when in the movement of the suffragettes these sufferings and sentiments were integrated, thus contributing to the recasting of our views concerning the place and function of women in modern society. In the same way the dissatisfactions of the oppressed classes (such as serfs, slaves, workers) were socially irrelevant as long as they remained the isolated experience of individuals. It was only when these sentiments were integrated into a movement which not only tried to express bitterness but attempted to formulate a basis of constructive criticism that the random feelings and actions were transformed into social functions.

This example sufficiently shows that only through specific forms of integration can latent reserves be mobilized and creatively integrated into society. When dealing with the significance of Youth for society, it is equally important to ask what is the nature of that potential that Youth represents, and through which forms of integration this reserve can be transformed into function. Or, to put it quite simply: What do we really mean by saying that Youth is a revitalizing agent?

Immediately a pitfall awaits us. When I was young it was the current belief that Youth is progressive by nature. This has since proved to be a fallacy, since we have learned that conservative or reactionary movements can also build up Youth movements. If we state that Youth is a revitalizing agent in social life, it will be advisable to point quite clearly to those elements in adolescence which, if mobilized and integrated, help society to make a new start.

From our point of view, the most important asset of Youth in helping to make a new start in society is that, apart from its greater spirit of adventure, it is not yet completely involved in the *status quo* of the social order. Modern psychology and sociology of the adolescent [3] have taught us that the key to the understanding of the mentality of modern Youth cannot alone be found in the biological fermentation of this stage of human development. After all, this is universal and restricted neither in place nor time. The decisive fact about the age of puberty from our point of view is that Youth at this age enters public life, and in modern society it is then that they are for the first time confronted with the chaos of antagonistic valuations. It has been proved that in primitive societies the mental conflicts of our Youth are unknown, for there is no radical cleavage between the norms taught by the family and those prevailing in the world of the grown-ups. The greater conflict-consciousness of our Youth is only the reflection of the chaos that prevails in our public life, and the bewilderment which ensues is a natural reaction of the inexperienced mind. For our discussion it is not so much the greater conflict-consciousness of Youth which is relevant but rather another facet of the very same situation in which they find themselves. In the context of our problems the relevant fact is that Youth come to the conflicts of our modern society from without. And it is this fact which makes Youth the predestined pioneer of any change in society.

Youth is neither progressive nor conservative by nature, but is a potentiality which is ready for any new start. Up to the age of puberty the child lives mainly in the family and his attitudes are mostly shaped by the emotional and intellectual traditions which prevail there. In the period of adolescence he makes his first contacts with the neighbourhood, the community and certain

spheres of public life. Thus the adolescent is not only biologically
in a state of fermentation, but sociologically he penetrates into a
new world where the habits, customs and value systems are
different from what he has known so far. What to him is a
challenging novelty is in the grown-up already habitualized and
taken as a matter of course. Then this penetration from without
into society makes Youth especially apt to sympathize with
dynamic social movements which, for reasons mostly different
from his, are dissatisfied with the existing state of affairs. Youth
has no vested interests yet, either in an economic sense or in terms
of habits and valuations, whereas most of the settled adults have.
This is the explanation of the peculiar fact that in their adolescence and prolonged adolescence so many people are ardent
revolutionaries or reformers, whereas very often the very same
people, as soon as they accept a settled job and found a family, are
on the defensive and plead for the *status quo*. In the language of
sociology being young mostly means being a marginal man, in
many respects an outsider. Indeed, the outstanding fact about
the attitude of schoolboys of higher forms and young students is
that they have as yet no vested interests in the existing social order
and have not yet integrated their contribution into the economic
and psychological fabric of existing society. In my view, this
outsider position is a more important factor than biological fermentation in making for changeability and openness, and it tends
to coincide with the outsider attitudes of other groups and individuals who for other reasons live on the fringe of society,[4] such as
oppressed classes, the unattached intellectuals, the poet, the artist,
etc. Of course, this outsider situation is a potentiality only and,
as I said, it depends very largely on the management and guiding
influences coming from outside whether this potentiality will be
suppressed or will be mobilized and integrated into a movement.

To sum up briefly the results of our general analysis: Youth
is an important part of those latent reserves which are present in
every society. It depends on the social structure whether those
reserves, and which of them, if any, are mobilized and integrated
into a function. The special factor which makes the adolescent
the most important asset for a new start in society is that he or she
does not take the established order for granted and has no vested
interests either in its economic or in its spiritual order. Finally,
static or slowly changing traditional societies do without the

mobilization and integration of these resources. They will even be keen on suppressing these potentialities, whereas a dynamic society is bound sooner or later to call to the fore these latent resources, and in many cases even organize them.

II. The Special Function of Youth in England in the Present Situation

If we try to apply this general analysis to the situation of Youth in English society to-day, we find all the symptoms we mentioned as being characteristic of a static, traditional society. Up to the present, the educational system, in spite of many valid criticisms of it, is an expression of the traditionalism prevailing in this country. Similarly, the very unobtrusive rôle Youth has played in it is in accordance with this evolutionary character. Whereas one can understand and even approve of the fact that English society was in the past over-cautious concerning Youth as it did not want to release its dynamic potentialities, my contention is that in the future this society can neither win the war nor the peace unless it gives scope to all the vital and spiritual resources which are at its disposal, and among them mainly the potentialities latent in Youth.

If this war is a war of ideas and a war of different social systems, it can only be won if we have constructive ideas. Not only ideas in the abstract but real inner reconstruction is needed, which will transform the existing social and political system and lead it to a higher form of democracy than that which was adjusted to the needs of the nineteenth century. Much as I appreciate those latent moral resources which have carried the war so far— toughness, self-control, social conscience, solidarity—they will not suffice unless they are supplemented by ideas and a desire for a better world. Even if one should take the line that, to the English, unconscious impulses are more important than ideas and conscious motivations, I am sure that without a creative vision, without the help of the pioneering spirit of Youth, neither the subjugated peoples of Europe nor the more dynamic masses in the U.S.A. will be ready to sacrifice everything they possess, their labour, their wealth and their lives.

If this were true, the fact that this country remains so in-articulate when it comes to the formulation of ideas might make us despair. But one has only to look at the great institutional changes that now occur one after the other, and one will realize that the prevailing silence is by no means a symptom of stagnation. Looking at these facts, one can certainly say that, under the pressure of war, changes are taking place which, if consciously guided, might be developed into a new type of society, a society which could integrate into a new pattern the advantages of planning with the freedom of a democratic order. By making the necessary adaptations to the needs of war one does not always realize that very often they contain also the principles of adaptation to the needs of a New Age. All of us know by now that from this war there is no way back to a laissez-faire order of society, that war as such is the maker of a silent revolution by preparing the road to a new type of planned order.

This is one of the lessons to be learnt from war economy: that business and finance at least as much as health services or social work are public activities, and if they are left in private hands it can only be as long as their management proves more efficient than a collective one.

This is another of the lessons to be learnt from war economy: ownership of capital and private profits can to a certain extent be admitted, but they must be controlled whenever they become antagonistic to public interest.

And here, again, is a lesson to be learnt from war economy: that it is not one of the "sacred rights of the individual" to invest his money and to speculate *ad libitum*, but that the decisions on crucial issues must fit in with a comprehensive plan.

And this, finally, is a lesson from war economy: that if we accept the principle that we can plan social change, social revolutions can be brought about peacefully, as long as we agree that those who lose by these inevitable changes must be compensated or re-trained for new functions, and those who unduly gain from changes must be heavily taxed.

What is developing in all the present changes is, so far, neither Fascism nor Communism; it may become a Third Way, the new pattern of planned society which, although using the techniques of planning, maintains its democratic control, and keeps those spheres of freedom and free initiative which are the genuine safeguards of culture and humanity. All this is in the making, yet nobody dares to proclaim its truth, nobody sets down its principles or broadcasts its idea to the world. Many are aware that certain steps taken in the wrong direction may eventually lead to Fascism. But there is in the country the readiness to sacrifice and, more than elsewhere, the determination to pay the price for the peaceful development of a New Order which will make life once more worth living. But this determination finds hardly any adequate expression on the ideological plane. The world is longing for a new pattern of social reconstruction. In Britain it is in the making in fits and starts; yet it may completely fail in the end, or if it succeeds it may fall short of its grandeur, because one has not the courage to express the idea which is already at work on it. If circumstances were less urgent, one might well say: "Let the necessary happen and do not talk about it," if that should make the birth of the new world more tolerable to those to whom it means sacrifice. But at the present juncture, when the finding of the new forms of control is hampered by obsolete concepts of liberties, it is a question of survival whether we are able to develop a new social philosophy which interprets the meaning of events to the community and to the world at large. So far, nothing of the kind has happened. In a completely changing world Britain tries to go on by adjusting herself only materially without adjusting herself spiritually to the new situation.

If this be true, there is nothing more urgent than to find out the deeper causes of this frustration in the spiritual field. As the mobilization of the latent spiritual resources will be one of the tasks of Youth, it will be necessary to describe more concretely the nature of that frustration, even if this compels us to dwell on some unpleasant features.

If one comes from the Continent, one of the striking facts about this country is the peculiar deprecation of theory and general ideas. Nearly every conversation with a certain type of educated person will sooner or later lead to utterances such as this: "We English dislike principles, abstract thoughts and ideas. We prefer to muddle through. We dislike theory. We are inarticulate and wish to be so." Notwithstanding the positive aspects of this matter-of-factness, of that tendency towards concreteness in a world submerged in an inflation of words and meaningless symbols, there is somewhere a limit to its efficiency. The hatred of theory is discredited if at the same time we see the admission of cranks with their pet theories. But this paradox arises only because, if a social system does not admit theory in its proper place, the latter is bound to slip in through the back door. The dislike of general ideas proves to be very often a kind of perversion in those to whom it is an excuse for avoiding dealing with the most important issues ahead. Those who are reluctant to discuss the basic principles of peace aims [5] and of social reconstruction are mostly not doing so because it is too early for such discussion as they pretend, but because they are afraid of touching upon anything that calls for creative imagination and constructive thought. In any other situation there may be a good excuse for their reluctance to think ahead. At the present juncture they prevent the growth of that fermentation which alone is able to carry the war effort and to make the life and death struggle an inspiring issue.

Fortunately this habit of mind which shrinks from theory and dynamic ideas is not a "racial" characteristic of the English, but a product of specific social classes in a historical and sociological configuration which is now coming to its end.

The ideology of the hatred of abstract ideas and of theory was most clearly laid down by Edmund Burke in his reaction to the French Revolution. In many ways his attitude adequately expressed a mood which became very widespread in the English educated classes. It was accepted because it was in conformity with the type of adjustment to change which has long prevailed in this country. But even if up to the present this attitude was partly justified, the exaggerated adherence to it now might become too dangerous, when only those nations seem to survive which are quick enough to realize the radical changes taking place in the social structure, and which are able to produce a new pattern in keeping with the new situation. However respectable those virtues are which go with the traditional type of adjustment, they will, in their exclusive appeal to unconscious emotions and habits, neither solve those problems of modern life where hard thinking is needed, nor be understood by those peoples which are craving for a lead and for a creative vision of the future social order. And after all, this call for greater articulateness does not mean the abandonment of tradition where it is alive. It means rather the removal of some social handicaps from which the frustration originates. If the deeper sources of that mental frustration which prevent ideas from taking their proper place in English society are sociological in nature, my analysis will remain incomplete unless I enumerate at least some of them. Thus, in what follows I shall enumerate six of the main sociological causes making for this frustration.

(1) There is the great security and wealth, partly due to the insular situation, partly to the unchallenged primacy of Britain in the world, which made it possible that social transformation should be brought about through tradition and gradual reform. As long as this lasted, it was sufficient to deal with social maladjustments one by one in a purely hand-to-mouth fashion. No systematic thinking, no awareness of general principles was needed as long as the broader framework of society could be taken for granted and only the details had to be filled in.

(2) Another source of the British reluctance to think ahead, to listen to ideas which try to state the direction of social change, is the presence of an influential rentier-class. In France and in this country it was their over-anxiousness and complacency which built Maginot lines wherever possible; it was the mentality which did not want to face Hitlerism as a completely new system and as a menace. Hitler's power and influence could have been broken if only its significance had been realized in time. But to think ahead, to realize the entire novelty of the challenge would have meant the voluntary acceptance of higher taxation on the one hand and a disturbance of their peace of mind on the other. Wherever the rentier-mentality prevails, their unconscious fears will kill the imagination and the courage to investigate into the meaning of change. In a static and satiated society this slowness may be a safeguard against risky experiments, but when everything is fluid and risk is so big that security becomes an illusion, it is only through creative imagination and constructive thought that the entirely changed situation can be diagnosed.

(3) A third source of this inarticulateness is that the Englishman lives more in his institutions than in reflective thought. Parliamentary institutions, local government, voluntary associations, habits, customs, manners, pageantry, etc., are well-established forms of activity in which a definite kind of spirit is embodied. If one sticks to the procedures as they are prescribed in institutions, the spirit is present without making it imperative that those who act should always be conscious of the meaning of these procedures. One is democratic because the institutions are

democratic or because democracy is a way of life. In many respects it is the ideal way of having assimilated democracy by possessing it in terms of practice and not only on the level of abstractions. Yet when it comes to sudden changes which call for complete readjustment or when it is important that the world should understand the meaning of these changes, these bigger issues can only be achieved in the medium of ideas.

(4) A fourth source of the disparagement of ideas can be found in the widespread disparagement of those who produce them, of the free-lance intelligentsia. Of course, intellectuals in this country are not prevented from uttering their views. There is politically and in other respects far-reaching freedom to express opinion and criticism. But the intellectuals are more or less regarded as a foreign body in the nation. They are either somehow looked down upon, spiritually isolated, or not really taken seriously. One has only to read the "Letters to the Editor" which appeared in *The Times* some time ago under the heading "The Highbrow." They show that the main aspect under which the intelligentsia appear to the public is simply one of irritation. The man in the street who would like to believe that everything in the world could be settled in the terms of habit and routine feels irritated by the existence of a group which wishes to go beyond that. In this case, the source of the disparagement of ideas and of the man who lives on having ideas is not only the rentier-class but also the "practical" business man and certain groups among civil servants. They all dislike ideas and the intelligentsia, because they fail to see that, in spite of their many shortcomings, small circles of the intelligentsia, by virtue of their being outsiders in society, are the main source of fermentation and dynamic imagination. The truth is that only those who are less bound in their imagination by office or vested interests can really be productive in that realm which goes beyond the boundaries of specialism and partisanship.

(5) The whole educational edifice, with its emphasis on examinations, marks, memorizing, or inventories of facts, is busy killing the spirit of experimentation so vital in an epoch of change. Besides, the exclusion of sociological knowledge from the educational curriculum of universities and secondary schools is a dangerous method of discouraging thinking about the decisive issues of the day. The traditional methods of teaching had their

justification as long as their main function was to create the spirit of basic conformity and that readiness for reproductive adjustment which goes with a static society. But the very same methods become an impediment to the understanding of the world in transition if they hamper the spirit of adventure and of creative adjustment to unforeseen experience. To-day it is becoming evident that it is impossible to expect a democracy to survive if the science of society is neglected in it, both as an aid to those who govern and to those who have to judge their achievements as parts of a coherent scheme of reform. The times are past when small minorities could base the perpetuation of their rule on the ignorance of the bulk of the population. The uneducated and uninformed masses to-day are a greater danger to the maintenance of any order than classes with a conscious orientation and reasonable expectations. The age of a tacit consensus within the ruling classes which did not want to give away the rules of thumb of government is gone, and those who want to keep the lower classes uneducated mostly fail to live up to the new achievements of sociological knowledge, which alone give orientation in an entirely changed and highly complex environment.

(6) The last, but perhaps the most important, cause of the prevailing frustration in the spiritual field is linked up with the fact that in this country Youth has not got its proper place and share in public life. This is also in accordance with the traditional pattern of society. There, the neutralization rather than a mobilization of the psychological resources of Youth was the hidden aim. But for our society it is a question of life and death whether reorganization can be carried out in time. Its very survival depends upon whether a new start can be made by those age-groups which have not yet vested interests in existing habits and valuations and are free to identify their emotions and enthusiasm with the new problems of their community. Only those to whom the problems of a new life are a real challenge will bring inspiration into a world of routine. In the Victorian era of traditional society, the vestiges of which are still present, the neutralization of the spiritual forces latent in Youth occurred in two ways. First of all, prestige in society was mainly with the elderly, and therefore their mentality prevailed. Secondly, in the absence of spontaneous Youth associations, the peculiar spirit of Youth and its peculiar qualities

could not integrate, and therefore did not contribute to the dynamics in society. In a society where a person grows shaped mainly by family attitudes, and apart from them only knows the abstract and impersonal attitudes of public life as they are met with in the office, in the workshop, in business or politics, something, and that the most important social ferment, will be lacking. The community spirit and the attitudes which underlie it are best acquired during adolescence in the gangs of youngsters. It is here that man learns to understand the self-regulating powers of spontaneous group life and the spirit of solidarity. If the potentialities of the gang-age remain unused, the self-centredness of the individuals will run amuk, an atomization of society will follow, isolation and exaggerated craving for privacy will torment the individual. The repression of the craving for communal experience in adolescence, when it is strongest, will at a later stage lead to an exaggerated competitiveness.

The public schools, of course, through their boarding system create an opportunity for this gang experience, but one can hardly say that they sufficiently foster the self-regulating powers of spontaneous group life. They seem rather to be anxious to superimpose rules of artificial rigidity upon that natural self-equilibrium, in order to inculcate the spirit of hierarchy, submission and other virtues of social cohesion which are mainly needed for the self-perpetuation of a ruling minority. Whereas in a real democracy the gang-age should be used for the real interpenetration of various classes, for the creation of a nation-wide basic conformity and unity, the public schools as they are rather serve the idea of segregation and group seclusion.

The real problem, therefore, seems not so much to be whether they should be preserved or abolished, but how and in which inner state of mind they should be preserved. This much seems evident: in the boarding system and in so many other features of their traditions they have preserved virtues which want to be socialized rather than extirpated.

But this "socialization" and transfer of group virtues to other classes cannot be brought about by institutional regulations alone. A thorough scrutiny of the educational methods prevailing in these schools will also be necessary. Each item of their method and of the habit system will have to pass the test of whether it is of lasting value and adapted to the new needs of the community.

Once one has decided for the maintenance of these schools for the sake of their cultural heritage, the problem of the assimilation of the newcomers from the ascending classes will become a problem which has equally to be faced in the light of conscious scrutiny. In the new type of evolutionary democracy which does not believe that it is best to start from scratch, as the past is not just considered to be the cumulation of outlived habits, the problems of preventing the process of levelling down cultural standards is a very serious one. One can be a very good democrat, or a Socialist, and still admit that too rapid an expansion of culture may lead to an inadequate assimilation of its contents, to superficiality and a rapid decline of established standards. Both Mass Democracy and Totalitarianism show that this really happens; that democratization of culture will benefit mankind only if the quality of culture is preserved. If this fails to happen, it is not the socially lower classes that are to be blamed but those who failed to realize that sudden admission of the many to the benefits of culture has carefully to be prepared both in the educational and the social field. Far from believing that the "lower classes" are less apt by nature to become the heirs of culture, it is only too evident that their unjust exclusion from the benefits of a proper education keeps them in a state of mind which can become a menace to the quality of culture. Gaining equal rights from one day to the next, they will naturally tend to make their prevailing taste predominant and will superimpose their wishes upon the gasping minority of the educated few. The problems with which the B.B.C. is confronted give a miniature picture of what happens in the larger arena of a mass democracy day by day. If it followed the wishes of the many, the variety programmes would gradually suppress classical music and everything else. The answer to this is not to speak contemptuously of the masses, but to consider the fact of the social and cultural rise of the ascending classes as a problem of social strategy in which primary and secondary schools (including the public schools), universities, adult education, etc., have their rôle to play.

In this scheme the rôle of the public schools should certainly be to act both as the preservers of the valuable elements in the cultural inheritance and also as the recipients of that fresh stimulus and vitality which seems always to be the quality of rising classes. The sudden opening of new opportunities for groups which have for centuries lived under immense pressure elicits a kind of new *élan* lacking in classes which have lived in wealth and security for centuries. It is therefore not quite adequate to say that the main task of the public schools should be to broaden the social basis of selection and thereby simply to assimilate the best from the rising classes, but that they must establish a living relationship of give-and-take among the adolescents of different social strata. From this angle it is a most inspiring task to make use of the gang-age and its potentialities as a source of new social synthesis and spiritual regeneration of a new era. If the public schools, instead of developing into a stronghold of privilege, become aware of this mission and live up to it, their contribution will be indispensable in the reconstruction of our social order and in the creation of new life.

III. MAIN CONCLUSIONS

This is the historical and sociological background to the situation in which Britain finds herself, and this is the background against which the problem of Youth has to be discussed at the present moment. What is really happening in this country is that the social pattern of a commercial democracy on the defensive is to be transformed into a militant democracy ready to give a lead to social reconstruction and to the reorganization of the world order in a completely new spirit. Nothing less than this can be aimed at in the present situation, and it does not rest with us to remain humble and to devote ourselves only to smaller parochial tasks. It is a question of survival whether we can achieve the greatest of all goals, i.e. the birth of the new social order out of the traditions of democratic life. This task remains, whatever the outcome of the war may be, because the struggle between totalitarianism and democracy will go on for the next generation at least. As to the question of what Youth can give us, the answer is: It is one of the most important latent spiritual resources for the revitalization of our society. It must become the pioneering force in a militant democracy. Within the country its task is to break down that mental frustration which, as we have seen, is very often willing to make a sacrifice in the material field but is unwilling to formulate the idea of a change which is in the making before our eyes. Outside the country its task is to become the pioneer who carries the idea into a world which is craving for a solution of the social problem.

If this pioneering function is to be assumed by our Youth it can only be achieved in a nation-wide movement.[6] As I pointed out previously, the latent forces of a nation can only be mobilized if they are integrated. A static society can afford to let the age of puberty pass unnoticed, without really achieving integration through a unifying purpose and without charging it with a historical function. But a dynamic society cannot do without this greatest asset in the spiritualization of its objectives. If those who will have to live within the new order, those who have to disseminate its idea—in fact, Youth—are not moved by it, the coming social reconstruction will mean nothing but a set of new regulations decided above the heads of the people. If Youth is really to become a pioneer for the new cause, only a nation-wide policy of Youth will help us. That means that we have to set free that spontaneous fermentation which is taking place all over the country, encourage its integration into a broad stream, and give Youth a fair chance to become helpers in a comprehensive movement working at current tasks and for social reconstruction. This integral Youth policy will, of course, not be limited to the fostering of a nation-wide Youth movement; it will also have to affect our whole educational system, as the latter will have to assist in educating a whole generation for entirely new tasks.

I know that at a first hearing all this sounds as if I were imitating the methods of the totalitarian states in their dealing with Youth. But what I should like to bring home is that there is a way of learning from events, and even from our opponents, which is the exact opposite of imitation. I think there are two possibilities of blind imitation in relation to the techniques used by our enemy. The first consists in slavish imitation of whatever they do. This is mostly prompted by hidden fears which suggest to us that they are somehow always right. But there is another form of imitation, which has been called negative imitation, when we refuse to learn from anything the enemy does because we want to have our own way at any price. Now, I think this attitude is equally slavish, as in this case we do not analyse methods and techniques on their own merits, but always with an eye to whether our enemy uses them or not. As contrasted with this, the real independence of our mind can only be preserved if we rely upon our own judgment as to the merits of an institution, and admit that many items in our opponents' methods are simply a response to a changed situation which affects us equally, whereas other items are simply due to his philosophy of life, which is not ours, and which we therefore refuse to accept.

To apply this distinction to the problem of Youth in modern society : the fact that the totalitarian states have tried to organize the entire Youth of their nation and to put the latent potentialities of Youth at the service of the community has nothing to do with their special philosophies of life, but with the fact that they became dynamic. The Youth movement, the realization that Youth should be one of the most important pioneers in building up a new world, is nothing but an expression of a dynamic society under modern conditions which is mobilizing all its resources in the service of a new social ideal. In the same way, the idea of a consistent, all-round Youth policy, which of course equally affects education as such, is also the necessary product of a society which has made up its mind to build up a new social order and no longer wants to build it in fits and starts and in terms of improvization. Thus, if Britain wants to transform her traditional pattern of democracy on the defensive into a dynamic society, she will also have to make use of Youth as pioneers for her cause.

Up to this point we must travel for a while on the same path as any other dynamic society. The difference comes at the point where our ideas on social reconstruction and our methods of achieving social aims differ from those of the totalitarian states.

It is obvious that this country is groping her way towards a new type of planned society which is neither Fascism nor Communism but a new stage in the history of industrial society, which eliminates all those elements that make for chaos in laissez-faire Liberalism, without at the same time abolishing the great achievements of liberty and democratic control. This country is seeking a solution which brings security and greater social justice, without displacing from political leadership those who are willing to co-operate in a more moderate but perhaps less hazardous plan for social reconstruction. A transformation like this, if it wants to avoid the supremacy of one party, can be built upon a pledge between different parties to support the long-range changes on which they have agreed. But the very same pledge must contain all the guarantees that the agreed reform will be carried out under the control of Parliament. In this assembly one will have to watch even more carefully than before the maintenance of those types of freedom which are compatible with that minimum of centralization and organization without which a mass society, based upon large-scale industrial technique, could not work at all. A social programme on these lines is bound to have an appeal in an age which has seen the deterioration of the radical methods and is craving for a social transformation the price of which is neither dictatorship nor the rule of terror and a relapse into barbarism.

So much must suffice as to the idea, and we can leave it at that, all the more as this time we are more interested in the method which will characterize the Third Way. The method is important because it will to a large extent determine the spirit, the values and the practices of our Youth movement and our educational system. As the political method of transformation will be reformist and not revolutionary, as nothing like the idea of class war or racial war or imperialist war will have to capture the minds, the pattern of education and the spirit of the Youth movement will have to be developed accordingly.

In the common-experience groups of adolescence the spirit of solidarity and co-operation will be aimed at. Not authoritarianism and the idea of irreconcilable differences, but mutual understanding will be the ideal. But this peace-loving, compromising spirit will differ in one respect from the education for tolerance as it prevailed in the age of laissez-faire. We shall not confuse tolerance with neutrality as to right and wrong. This is the reason why I spoke of a militant democracy. What we have learned from the bitter experiences of the last decades is that the meaning of democratic tolerance is not to tolerate the intolerant, but that the citizen of our commonwealth has a perfect right to hate and to exclude those who wish to misuse the methods of freedom for abolishing freedom. Unlike the brutal wholesale regimentation of dictatorships who allow only one cast of thought and action, equally unlike the passive abstention of laissez-faire Liberalism from taking any side at all, this militant democracy will have the courage to come out into the open for certain basic values common to all; yet it will, on the other side, leave the more complicated values to free individual choice and decision.

This balance between agreed conformity and freedom may sound strange to those who have devoted their whole life to the idea of progressive education. They will have to remember that at present not only the conservatives are at the cross-roads, but the progressives are so too. In an age of planning, the method of being a partisan and nothing else has to undergo a change. In this light it is necessary to realize that our progressive educational movements, with many of the experimental schools, were compelled by historical circumstances to represent the opposition in society. That means that their historical function was always to emphasize the method of freedom. They tried to prove that much more can be achieved by the method of freedom than by the method of command; they pointed out the dangers of inculcation, repression and blind obedience, and emphasized the powers of spontaneity, creativeness and free experiment. The advantage of being in opposition is that one has not to take responsibility for the whole of the social fabric. They could carry the methods of freedom to their utmost limits without being afraid that the whole building of society might collapse. They could do so as there were sufficient forces of tradition and authority to prevent their method being put to a final test. They were in the position of the early Christians who, although they fought against the Roman Empire, prayed in secret for its existence, because, after all, it alone made their own existence possible.

But if that partisan thinking, or thinking for one polarity only, is to cease, if in a planned society we shall have to learn to think for and on behalf of the whole, we shall have to correct our partisan approach, and the very same people who have so far pleaded for the new forms of freedom only, will equally have to care for the new forms of authority.

Our next task will be to experiment with new forms of authority in our communities and common-experience groups. We have to find new forms of authority which are based neither wholly upon blind obedience nor on that gradually emerging spontaneous group experience which is the ideal of radical liberals or anarchists. There must be forms of authority in between these two extremes which, on the one hand, do not kill spontaneity and intelligent insight but which, on the other, are workable in Great Society in which we cannot always wait till spontaneous consensus leads to a decision. That waiting for the latter may become disastrous could be seen in Britain and recently in the United States. Hitler thrives on that delay which was caused by the slowness of the democratic countries in coming to a decision. I think the solution to this difficulty will be found in the formula that there is no single remedy. The choice is not between absolute freedom and blind obedience. On the contrary. There are shades and grades between these two extremes; there are issues on which complete agreement is needed, and others where absolute obedience is imperative, and between these two lie those issues in relation to which blended attitudes alone work. The Nazis base their whole educational system on one-sided behaviour: training for hatred, training for blind obedience, training for fanaticism. What a militant democracy has to aim at is to impart blended attitudes and the capacity to respond differently according to the challenge or the task at hand. By "blended attitudes" I understand a form of behaviour which is not driven from one extreme to the other, from violent hatred to submissive guilt feelings, from an inferiority feeling through over-compensation to a superiority complex, but which is proud of a balance of the mind which can only be achieved through self-control and intelligence.

I have no doubt that blended attitudes can be imparted if we educate for them. This is possible, and this country is really great in producing the balanced mind and blended attitudes. Here self-control and equanimity are compatible with toughness and fighting spirit. Sound scepticism is compatible with unquestioned belief in some basic virtues. If we believe that the Nazi method is only the more primitive type of upbringing, then it is only a matter of real exertion on our part and a question of further educational experiments to define and elaborate the methods which suit our purposes.

In the same way, there is a third solution to the exaggerated antithesis: Shall we educate for group conformity or shall we foster the growth of an independent balanced personality? The answer is to be found in a kind of gradualism. Education by degrees: first for group conformity and then for the emergence of the many-faceted, balanced personality. Of course, by these degrees I do not exactly mean sequences of time, but stages in using methods which gradually lead both to the creation of group responses and to emancipated attitudes. It is obvious that this balanced personality will not be achieved at once, and it is very likely that the ideal will not be reached by all the members of the community. But still, the main difference between an integrated Youth policy according to the democratic pattern and the totalitarian *Gleichschaltung* in the dictatorial states is that, whereas the latter through all its institutions and all its grades inculcates the same conformity, our system will develop an educational strategy in which on the lower levels basic conformity, cohesion, habit-making, emotional training, obedience will be developed, and on the higher levels a gradual emergence of those qualities will be fostered which make for individualization and the creation of independent personalities. To us group existence, loyalty to common issues and emotional solidarity will not be in contradiction to the emergence of an independent personality with critical powers of judgment. Our belief is that it is possible to create a pioneering and militant type which is not fanatical, an emotional type whose emotions are more than displaced fears, and that it is possible to train judgment through common-life experience and bring about obedience which is not blind, but a devotion to spontaneously believed ideals.

This new democratic personalism will differ from the atomistic individualism of the laissez-faire period in that it will restore the genuine powers of group life. It will achieve this, among other means, through the great attention it will pay to the gang-age and to the potentialities which are inherent in the self-regulating forces of group existence. It must become the meaning of a nation-wide Youth movement that it breaks down the frustration which comes from isolation, exaggerated privacy and sectarianism, and mobilizes instead the forces of group living in the service of a social ideal. But whereas the dictatorial state perverts these potentialities of primary group life into a training-ground for fanatic obedience and complete conformity,[7] the democratic utilization of group existence uses its powers for training a personality which can do both, co-operate in groups and remain a person of judgment and independence of mind.

In these concluding remarks I could not do more than point in the direction where my Third Way lies. But the task of an idea is exactly this: to mobilize the creative imagination for a new purpose. Once this is achieved, the details can be worked out through common experience. And for this common experience we have not to wait. We have got it on a world-wide scale. Thus we have to start here and now. The war has created a situation in which the basic conditions for finding the Third Way are present, and we all know that nothing can help but the co-operative effort of the whole nation gradually to elaborate the new pattern of society and that type of man who can show the way out of the present chaos and decay.

IV

EDUCATION, SOCIOLOGY AND THE PROBLEM OF SOCIAL AWARENESS

I. The Changing Features of Modern Educational Practice [1]

One of the most important changes in the educational field seems to be the gradual change from the compartmental concept of education, as it prevailed in the age of laissez-faire, to the integral concept. The first concept treated education as a more or less self-sufficient compartment of life. It thought in terms of schools and classes where teachers instructed boys and girls in subjects specified by the curriculum. The progress of the students, and indirectly the capacity of the teacher, was assessed by a system of marks. There were written examinations, and if these were passed to the satisfaction of the examining body, the aim of education had been achieved. Some may consider this to be a caricature, but others will blame me for characterizing this method as belonging to the past only. They may feel that too many still act and think in these terms. However this may be, even if it is a caricature, it represents in an exaggerated form the tendency towards compartmentalization.

Education was a compartment because the school and the world had become two categories not complementary but rather opposed to each other. Education was a compartment up to that age limit at which a human being was expected to be accessible to educational influence. Up to a certain age educational institutions tried to impress you and to impress your behaviour, whereas after the age limit you were free. This tendency towards compartmentalization has been broken by the revolutionary concept of adult education, extramural education, refresher courses, which familiarized us with the idea of post-education and re-education. It is equally due to the healthy influence of adult education that we acknowledge the fact that education ought to go on for life, that society is an educational agent, and that education at school is good only if in many ways it embodies the educational technique of life. From now on, the aim of the school is not only to impart ready-made knowledge but to enable us to learn more efficiently from life itself.

But it is not only getting rid of the bookish scholastic concept of learning which abolishes the barriers between school and life. The same tendency works equally strongly in other directions. In former days there was an absolute cleavage between home and school. Now attempts are made to bring together parents and teachers and to co-ordinate influences coming from school with those coming from home. The growth of social work, the study of juvenile delinquency, threw new light upon the share that various compartments of life have in the building of the character of the young. It became evident that if the home, the school, the child guidance clinic, the social worker, the juvenile court work only for themselves, they disregard each others' influence; thus a tendency to integrate their work was bound to follow.

But this realization of the need for integration in life had its influence on the work of the school in a different way. It led to an integral concept of the curriculum. This can best be shown in our changing concept of moral education. Formerly the moral self was to remain compartmentalized, and one thought to have paid due tribute to it if one inserted into the curriculum religious or moral education. To-day we know that this religious or moral education is bound to remain ineffective unless it is related to the other parts of the curriculum. Everything we teach, and even more how we teach it, has an impact upon character formation. Whereas formerly we thought that the mysteries of character training could be solved by games or the boarding-school system, to-day we know that the kind of games one plays and the intimate details of school organization are more important than the actual labels given to these games or school systems. The social organization of the school, the kind of social rôles one has an opportunity to play, whether competition or co-operation prevails, whether there is more opportunity for team work than for solitary work, all contribute to the type of man which will grow up in these surroundings.

These integrating trends in the curriculum are themselves nothing but an expression of a deeper psychological insight, namely that personality is one and indivisible. If we give up the previous rigid concept of school subjects and try to relate the knowledge gained in one course to that of other courses, it is because we know to-day that only a co-ordinated attack on the mind of the individual will be effective. The efficacy of our teaching depends on how we relate new experience to the already existing background of the individual. Ultimately the ideal teaching of a human being would take into account the whole life-history of the individual and many of the social factors which operate on him apart from the school. Thus education is becoming integral in two respects: (a) by integrating its activities with the activities of other social institutions; and (b) with respect to the wholeness of the person.

But the peak of the integrating tendencies is reached when not only in our practice but also in our theory we plainly admit that education is only one of the many social agencies influencing human behaviour, and as such, whether we want it or not, always serves a social purpose and is deliberately aiming at moulding certain human types.

In the previous age, the age of Liberalism, educational practice was over-compartmental; the main shortcoming of its theory was that it was society-blind. It could not see, or did not want to admit, the existence of society as a relevant factor in human affairs. It did not want to assess the impact of society upon the aims and methods of education.

In its theory, liberal education insisted upon the statement that the basic values and the aims of education were eternal, and the final and exclusive purpose of education was the fostering of the free development of personality through the unhampered unfolding of innate qualities. The integral theory of education, in its sociological aspects, does not object to that theory as such; it does not doubt the fact that some ideals may be stated which survive the ages and are the basis of any decent way of life and social organization. What it objects to is that this theory is too aloof from history to be really helpful in concrete situations. Whoever tries to state such eternal values very soon realizes that they are bound to be too abstract to lend concrete shape to education at a given moment. In the same way, if the final core of the self is something that is eternal and beyond environmental influence, we still have to consider that more empirical and historical attire in which we meet our fellow-beings as citizens of a given state, as workers in factories, as clerks in an office, as human beings striving for such satisfactions as are available in a given social order.

II. Some Reasons for the Need of Sociological Integration in Education

Our fathers and forefathers could do without sociological theories, for the interdependence between the institutions and human activities in a village or small community were too obvious and could be seen by everybody. In the age of our forefathers sociology was on the whole a part of common sense, but the immense growth of industrial society, the invisible operation of its forces, made society most enigmatic to the individual. Even the most careful observation of the immediate surroundings cannot disclose to the untrained mind what is going on beneath the surface, how effects accumulate and react upon each other.

The belief that one could settle the most important problems of education and social work on the basis of common sense alone was shaken whenever the different functionaries of society had to meet in connection with the same case. This revealed that the schoolmaster, the judge, the social worker, the public servant relied upon a completely different kind of common sense. The rule of thumb was different in the departments of administration, in education, the courts, etc., according to their peculiar traditions and the ideologies which prevailed in these circles. They very often held different views as to the effect of punishment, for instance, or assessed differently the effects of environmental influences upon the individual.

Fortunately, during the last decades a great deal of knowledge has been accumulated in the various branches of psychology and sociology. Child psychology, educational psychology, criminology, experimental psychology, psycho-analysis collected a whole store of material which was ready to be co-ordinated and integrated into a Science of Human Behaviour. From another angle sociology made its contribution to science. It observed man's behaviour in different societies, in primitive societies, in different phases of history, in different classes and in the social surroundings of our own society. It observed the effect of different social institutions such as the family, the community, the workshop, the gang, upon behaviour. It observed man under the conditions of social security, when he is craving for gradual improvement in his economic conditions, in his status or his enjoyment of leisure, but it also observed him under the conditions of social insecurity, social unrest, revolution and war.

Thus in the long run it became impossible to deal with the innumerable cases of personal and social maladjustment, as they followed from the growth of industrial society, disregarding that accumulated knowledge which characterizes human nature and its conditioning. This branch of sociology is another integrating link between the disciplines dealing with human affairs, and it is impossible to think of a teacher who does not, day by day, meet with behaviour difficulties in the child which, properly observed, are but symptoms of conflicts within the family, in the community, conflicts between age-groups, etc.

There is yet another sphere of sociological information which has to be acquired by the teacher, if his aim is not to educate his pupils in the abstract but for life in an existing society. As contrasted with those problems which grew out of the difficulties of the individuals to adjusting themselves to their immediate surroundings, there are maladjustments more comprehensive in scope. Here I have in mind the cultural crisis through which our society is passing, the spiritual changes in society at large, which certainly have their impact also upon the behaviour difficulties of individuals in their everyday life. I am thinking of those epoch-making changes caused by industrial civilization, such as the partial, sometimes total disorganization of our customs, habits and traditional valuations. I think of those social processes which very often disintegrate the family or the community. I think of the changed nature of work and leisure, and their impact upon personality formation or their disintegrating effects. I think of those tendencies in modern society which lead to a deterioration in our cultural life, to the lack of contact between the thinker, the artist and the community, the lowering of the standards by which we judge public affairs, the causes of the power of propaganda, the effects of commercialization, over-organization, etc. It is even more absurd that the teacher should be unaware of the sociological investigations concerning the place of Youth in modern society and of observations which show how biological fermentation and social unrest work together to create a generation which, if left to itself, will be unable to stand the strain of an age to come. In one word, it is impossible that the teacher should have no knowledge of these fundamental tendencies of deterioration, their causes and the remedies which have been tried with more or less success. It is impossible that we should return from the present war, the most inhuman in history, to peace-time conditions without having the assistance of the teachers in attacking these disintegrating tendencies. To-day no one can think of the peace after this war just as a going back to pre-war conditions. There will be too much upheaval and, therefore, an urgent need for a fundamental regeneration of our society. In the society of the past it was possible to hand down habits, customs and an established philosophy of life, which enabled the individual to play rôles in society which were more or less fixed in advance. In a changing society like ours only an education for change can help. The latter consists in an un-dogmatic training of the mind, which enables the person not to be driven by the current of changing events but to rise above them.

This is no longer possible through *ad hoc* improvised pseudo-sociological interpretations. There must be an informed mind which can discriminate between those genuine elements in the tradition which are still alive and make for emotional stability, and those human attitudes and institutions on the other side which decay because they have lost function and meaning in a changed society. It is our ignorance of the dehumanizing effects of industrial civilization upon the mind which allows the growth of that void into which the witch-doctors of propaganda pour their poison. If the modern teacher will think of himself not so much as a schoolmaster but as a lifemaster doing from another angle what the social worker does in his sphere, then he will be striving for all the knowledge available which could help him in this task. He will try to educate a generation of Youth which combines emotional stability with a flexible mind; yet he will only succeed if he is capable of seeing each of the problems of the new generation against the background of a changing world.

To sum up: we have so far met with sociology as an assistance to the teacher to overcome compartmentalization and the limited scholastic concept of education by orientating most of the things we teach to the needs of society. Then we met sociology as a help in co-ordinating the work of education with influences coming from institutions other than the school, i.e. from the family, the church, social work, public opinion, etc. We saw that the real meaning of education can only be assessed if its work is based upon a thorough study of human behaviour in its sociological aspects. Again, we met sociology as a help in interpreting many of the psychological conflicts and maladjustments of the individual as reflections of maladjustments in his immediate and the social surroundings. Finally, sociology appeared as a help in the understanding of the deeper sources of deterioration in our moral and cultural life, caused by the disintegration of tradition and the prevailing social structure. To express it in the language of academic subjects, courses on (1) Sociology of Education, (2) Science of Human Behaviour, (3) Sociology of Culture, (4) Study of Social Structure, ought to assist the training in education proper.

In all the functions analysed so far, sociology served as a help to make education more human, more social. We saw that in a modern, complex and quickly changing society education is only adequate if the teacher knows the social world from which his pupils come, for which they have to be prepared, and if he is capable of assessing most of the things he does in terms of social results. In all these aspects sociology is a necessary supplement to education in our age, in whatever country or in whatever social system we may live. The question emerges whether in addition to these services sociology has something special to give to education in this country and at this moment?

III. The Rôle of Sociology in a Militant Democracy

The same problem can be put in other words. Is there an aspect of sociology in which it not only gives information about isolated facts, certain causal sequences and trends, or is it also capable of giving, apart from surveys, descriptions or monographs, a synthetic picture of the present situation? Is there an integration of the empirical information available which can answer questions like these: "Where do we stand?" "Where do we go?" "Can sociology become an asset in framing our general policy?"

Before the outbreak of the war there would have been some obstacles in the way of accepting these synthesizing aspects of the teaching of sociology. One would gradually have admitted that some piecemeal information about society was a necessary subject in the curriculum, but one would have shrunk from drawing conclusions in terms of an approach aiming at a synthesis.

To-day there is nothing more obvious to thoughtful people than the need for a consistent and objective outlook concerning society and its present and future possibilities. The main difference between our pre-war democracy and the present one is that the former was a democracy on the defensive, which was mainly concerned with maintaining its equilibrium, whereas now we know that we can only survive if we are able to transform ourselves into a dynamic and militant democracy which will be capable of bringing about the necessary adjustments to the new situation from within, and at the same time express the nature of the changes required in terms of constructive ideas. These ideas must be true and timely and must appeal to the imagination of our younger generation, which has to fight for them, as well as to the peoples of the subjugated countries of Europe, who wait for such a lead.

One of the outstanding problems of the hour is, therefore, the lack of awareness in social affairs, which in one way is nothing but the lack of a comprehensive sociological orientation. Let me, therefore, make the question of awareness and of the causes of its suppression one of the main subjects of the following discussion.

By "awareness" I do not understand the mere accumulation of rational knowledge. Awareness means both in the life of the individual and in that of the community the readiness to see the whole situation in which one finds oneself, and not only to orientate one's action on immediate tasks and purposes but to base them on a more comprehensive vision. One of the ways in which awareness expresses itself is the correct diagnosis of a situation. An otherwise able Civil Servant may know all the technicalities which are needed to put into practice an administrative regulation, but he may be unaware of the configuration of the political forces which were responsible for the creation of the law and of the possible social effects that law will have on certain prevailing tendencies in society. These political and social realities lie in another dimension, beyond the range of his awareness. To give another example: A young man may be very clever, well trained

c*

and equipped for certain purposes, but still be quite unaware of those hidden anxieties which again and again interfere with his actions and defeat his purposes. By becoming aware of his psychological type or the deeper sources of his anxieties he gradually can gain control over factors which controlled him in the stage of unawareness. Awareness, therefore, is not measureable in terms of the acquired knowledge only, but in terms of the capacity of seeing the uniqueness of our situation and, let us add now, in terms of getting hold of facts which are on the horizon of our personal or group experience, but only enter into our consciousness through a special effort. This was the case of the young man who became aware of his unconscious fears. Awareness does not claim the knowledge of transcendental things which are beyond human experience, such as ghosts, spirits or even the divinity, but of facts which are ready to become part of experience yet do not enter into the picture because somehow we do not want to take cognizance of them.

To the real educationist this sphere of the knowable but not yet known should constitute a very important realm, worthy of his attention. My general attitude concerning the degree and quality of awareness is not that one should aim under all circumstances at the highest degree of awareness, but that it depends both on the situation of the individual and of a group, such as a nation, how much awareness is wanted, how much of it can be achieved and how it should be achieved.

Once more a simple example will make clear what I have in mind. An old peasant may be a wise man who by experience, by intuition and habit knows what he has to do in any given situation of life. Young peasant boys and girls may ask him for advice on all sorts of affairs of their lives concerning love, work, family, etc. He will always know how to deal with them, both in terms of custom, tradition and in terms of his own personal judgment. He will be able to give the right advice without being able consciously to define the whole situation in which he and his fellow-villagers live. The best test of his lack of awareness is that he will take it as a matter of course that the rules he applies are the rules of life in general and not only of the limited social world in which he happens to live. But an awareness of the situation might come to him as a revelation, if through a sudden removal from the village into a town he noticed that his wisdom and knowledge fail to cope with the new situation. First he would feel completely lost, not only because his habits and unconscious expectations are completely adjusted to a social world entirely different from the new one, but also because his ways of thinking and valuations are different from those which prevail in a town. His survival in the new surroundings will henceforth mainly depend on his ability to conform to their new demands, and this, in turn, will depend on his awareness. Awareness in his case will consist in the realization of the existence of two worlds side by side (the rural and the urban), each of which has its proper way of acting and thinking. That means that from now on most of the things he does must be accompanied by an awareness of the social frame of reference, by an awareness of the situation into which his responses will have to fit. This awareness will not hamper, as many people think, either his spontaneity or the development of his habits. Just the opposite holds true: awareness will assist him in reorganizing his behaviour and in reorientating his unconscious expectations.

But it is not only a change of environment which calls for awareness; any other change that leads to new conditions will make for a revision of habits, reorientation of expectations and for a search into the current changes. If an adolescent passes through the age of puberty and is being tormented by psychological and social conflicts, guidance consists in making him aware of the new situation. The very fact that he is able to define the situation in which he finds himself is very often an essential help in the search for a new equilibrium. In this connection it is not without interest to notice that if an adolescent passes through the age of puberty without developing the necessary awareness of that stage, it is very likely that he will be lacking in that quality up to the end of his life, although under specific conditions a kind of post-education even in this case may be of some help.

The need for awareness in society varies mainly with the rate of change and the nature of individual and group conflicts which go with it. As long as slow, gradual development and security prevail, there is no need for an excessive amount of awareness. If sudden changes occur, it is impossible to find the right way of action without reference to the meaning of change. Especially those who usually are expected to give lead to thought and action, the leaders in the various walks of life, will lose their followers if they are unable to define the situation anew. Sociology in terms of a thorough survey, a description of facts, will still be necessary in such an age of change, but the gist of its contribution will consist in a search into the new direction of events and into their new requirements.

Awareness is not to be mixed up with class-consciousness in the Marxian sense. Although the latter is a very important form of awareness it is only a special elaboration of it. Class-consciousness is awareness of those factors which make a social group or class ready to fight against another class or the rest of society covering up all other aspects of the whole situation. Class-consciousness deliberately blinds itself to those factors which, in spite of the prevailing conflicts, are making for cohesion and co-operation in society. Class-consciousness is the social world seen in the perspective of a fighting group.

Class-consciousness is partial awareness, whereas the awareness I have in mind is total awareness: awareness of the total situation, as far as that is humanly possible, at a given stage of history. It is a synthesis that emerges after the different aspects of partial group experiences have been confronted and integrated.

The specific feature of this country has been great security, wealth, gradual change. Thus there was no need for a continual revision of the situation, and social awareness could remain more or less undeveloped. It is only now that the rapid changes brought about by the war, and the even more rapid changes which will follow, make it a vital necessity that at least the leaders of the nation, and among them the teachers, should be educated in a way which will enable them to understand the meaning of change.

Whether under the pressure of changing events a complete psychological upheaval or reasonable reform will follow, depends mainly on whether there are leaders all over the country who are able to understand the situation in which they and their fellow-men find themselves, and whether they are able to present the pattern of reasonable adjustment. Where there is no reasonable pattern as an alternative to passing customs and habits in times of rapid change it is only natural that things go wrong and people go mad.

As awareness is not knowledge as such but an attitude of the mind, its development does not depend on instruction only but also on the removal of certain obstacles, such as unconscious fears. The resistance of almost all classes in this country to certain types of awareness is due not only to the happy continuity of its history which made possible a gradual adjustment to changing conditions, but also to a deliberate avoidance of every opportunity which might lead to a clear statement of the issues at stake. For this one cannot blame certain individuals or classes only. The conservatives were as responsible as those progressives who discussed pacifism when the enemy was at the gates. The appeasement policy of Chamberlain is just another feature of the same unwillingness to face unpleasant facts which prevailed in Labour circles who refused to rearm when they could have foreseen the results of unpreparedness. This artificially suppressed awareness has, of course, nothing to do with "race." It is simply a manifestation of continuity, of gradualness in change and a certain type of education which all together developed a style of life which no doubt has great beauty and aesthetic value. But the problem to me as a sociologist is not what is its worth in itself, but whether under the entirely changed conditions this suppressed awareness can last and, if not, what will happen to it. This question, however, can only be dealt with reasonably if we have still more detailed insight into the facts that have produced it.

I shall first mention two methods prevailing in academic teaching which largely contributed to the suppression in the educated classes of what we called awareness. Later, I shall enumerate some of the more comprehensive influences which used to work in the same direction.

The first academic method which produces that lack of awareness is over-specialization. It is a method of neutralizing the genuine interest in real problems and in the possible answers to them. Specialization is necessary in an age of highly developed differentiation, but if no effort is made to coordinate the pieces of specialized research and of the different subjects taught in the curriculum, this can only be due to the fact that such a synthetic picture is not wanted. The student is not only made unable to refuse dilettantish attempts at a synthesis, he is also rendered entirely uncritical by this method of teaching where everybody takes responsibility for a disconnected piece of research only and is, therefore, never encouraged to think of situations as a whole. Under present circumstances awareness is bound to rise and the craving for some coherent vision can no longer be completely suppressed: the great danger of the present situation, then, is that, without adequate training in the methods of synthesis, the students are bound to become an easy prey either of dilettanti or of propagandists who exploit that craving for their own or for their party's benefit.

Not only has the gradualness of change, the happy continuity of traditions, made it possible for this country to eliminate those situations in which issues become irreconcilable and therefore call for sharp definitions, but the very same social setting has developed a mental climate, a style of life which made it a principle to avoid not only overstatement but also any clear definition of the situation. If you come from the Continent one of the things that strike you most is that over here it seems to be a part of the accepted ways of life to leave many things unsaid which elsewhere would be plainly stated. Of course, if two Englishmen remain silent about certain things, both may know what is between the lines. But even so, it is characteristic that it is a dominant convention for many things to remain unsaid and to be present in the mind by implication only. Of course, I do not think now of sex, money and power, whose existence is not admitted by the conventions. One does not speak about them. But differences in opinion are rarely fought out in full, and hardly ever traced back to their final sources.

I admit the intrinsic value of this style of life, but I must also point to some of its disadvantages. In dealings with Continental Powers the non-committal language was very often misinterpreted. But an even greater danger of such a collectively suppressed awareness is that it may become suicidal by not realizing those current changes in the world at large which, if they remain unchallenged, turn against the nation. To-day we realize that during the last decades a collective delusion prevailed in this country which consisted in an attitude of first ignoring and then denying the existence of menacing facts such as the rise and the growth of the Fascist régimes in Italy and Germany. One simply did not want the collective peace of mind to be disturbed, and one ostracized men like Churchill

who dared to utter the truth. In that mood of suppressed awareness one denied also some of the other great changes taking
place in the world. In economics one did not want to admit
that the system of laissez-faire had run its course, that modern
organization needs co-ordination, that a certain amount of
planning is unavoidable, that a new type of State whose method
is mechanized robbery was becoming the adversary.

The other factor in our academic teaching which prevented
the growth of awareness was our misinterpretation of tolerance
and objectivity in terms of neutrality. Neither democratic
tolerance nor scientific objectivity demand that we should never
take a stand for what we believe to be true, nor that we should
avoid discussing the final values and objects of life.

But this was exactly what academic teaching used to aim at.
The treatment of subjects by democratic teachers was very much
like a carefully guided conversation in a drawing-room, where
everybody avoids issues which could lead to a passionate discussion in the search of truth.

It was exactly this kind of neutralization which brought about
a mental climate which from the very outset discouraged every
attempt to make a distinction between essential and non-essential
issues. The academic mind was proud of paying the greatest
possible attention to trifles and ridiculing those who wanted first
thing to come first. In this connection one has also to mention
the outlived educational principle that it does not matter what
you learn, and that you learn only for the sake of mental discipline—a statement to which the obvious answer would be:
Why should we not exactly for that reason acquire the mental
discipline on those subjects which really matter? The unconscious tendency to neutralize learning and the hidden desire
for self-frustration seems deliberately to avoid situations in which
one would be forced to learn the essential things and to take a
definite stand. This is as if one were to neglect the thorough
study of the geography of one's own country from fear lest the
enemy might possibly make use of the maps. The enemy will
study our geography anyhow. An education and training
which tries to prevent us from thinking about a subject in all
its ramifications and from taking a stand somewhere is bound
to create a human being incapable of offering real resistance
when life surrounds him with an arsenal of doctrines and

propaganda. When faced with the great issues of life, in his feeling of inferiority he will contemptuously call "clever" everybody who tries to find a solution, and he will develop a hatred of thinking in general, and avoid all discussions, an attitude which is essentially undemocratic. As long as there was no totalitarian enemy to challenge this country, neutralization of everything was just a waste of human energy. But once the opponent sets all his hopes on an ideological campaign the antidote to doctrine is better doctrine, not neutralized intelligence. It is here where the beginnings have to be made if we think that only militant democracy can win this war which, after all, is a war of ideas.

Of course, the militant attitude does not mean that totalitarian intolerance should take the place of free discussion, or that by removing the neutralizing effects of over-specialization we should neglect specialization altogether and should turn our teaching into propaganda. It only means that in the present situation no teaching is sound unless it trains man to be aware of the whole situation in which he finds himself, and that after careful deliberation he should be able to make his choice and come to a decision.

Apart from these merely academic methods of neutralizing the mind, there were other more fundamental causes at work. The deeper reason for pre-war democracy having avoided the creation of greater awareness was the fear that the discussion of vital issues might lead to a disintegration of that basic consensus which is a pre-condition of the functioning of democracy. Some fear this even more since the outbreak of the war, and this is the reason why they do not embark wholeheartedly upon the discussion of the problems of peace and post-war reconstruction. They are convinced that the discussion of these problems is bound to endanger that inner unity which is essential for the winning of the war. It is obvious that the people who think in these terms are caught on the horns of a dilemma. On the one hand, it is obvious that without constructive ideas they will neither inspire their own people nor those who suffer under the Fascist yoke. On the other hand, they frustrate the growth of the very same unifying ideas by being afraid of their possible effects. It is essential that we should face that issue honestly, and all the more so as our democracy, especially at the present juncture, can have a clear conscience, and has everything to gain and nothing to lose from growing awareness. When I am saying this I am not blind to the fact that it is essential both for the winning of the war and for the survival of democracy that the basic consensus should not be jeopardized. But the essential thing about true democracy is that differences in opinion do not kill solidarity as long as there is fundamental agreement on the method of agreement, i.e. that peaceful settlement of differences is better than one by violence. Democracy is essentially a method of social change, the institutionalization of the belief that adjustment to changing reality and the reconciliation of divers interests can be brought about by conciliatory means, with the help of discussion, bargaining and integral consensus.

This desire for consensus and a co-operative solution was not always quite evident in the different political parties and social groups before the outbreak of war, when too many thought that the basic dividing issue would be Capitalism—in the prevailing democratic or Fascist forms—on the one side and Communism on the other. This alternative was by many considered as irreconcilable: class war, dictatorship and complete annihilation of one's opponents seemed to have become the only methods of settling disputes.

Now my contention is that through the growth of Nazism and through the war the general situation has changed considerably. The main theme of history became different, and it is only due to a lack of awareness that all the parties still repeat their catch-phrases and do not dare to identify themselves entirely with the cause for which they make limitless sacrifice and for which they are already fighting. It is one of the remarkable features in history that the theme, the real *Leitmotif*, of its struggles may through circumstances change entirely, yet by remaining unaware of these changes people may still conceive of political alternatives in terms of their previous distinctions and antitheses. In this respect it is obvious that such great decisions as the outbreak of a world-wide war and the issues on which it is being fought have definitely a bearing on what will be experienced for a very long time to come as the fundamental theme of our struggles.

The great change of theme seems to be that whereas before the outbreak of war it looked as though the exclusive alternative

of the future would be that of Capitalism or Communism, since
the outbreak of war the dividing line for the Western countries
is freedom and democracy versus dictatorship. This, of course,
does not mean that the social question, the problem of social
reconstruction, has disappeared, but only that it ceased to be
predominant. This does not mean that we have reached the
happy state in which nothing is left of the former antitheses,
according to which we used to expect the demand for planning
and social justice to be on the one side, laissez-faire Capitalism
with industrial and financial leadership on the other.

The new fact is that the irreconcilability of this alternative
was mediated by an issue that seems to all the partners even
more important than their previous antithesis. That new over-
whelming issue is the maintenance of freedom and democratic
control. What is needed to make democracy safe is not the
exclusion of the social struggle, but that it should be fought
out by methods of reform.

Another factor that led to a mediation of the previous,
seemingly irreconcilable alternative was that in the very struggle
for victory the democratic state of Britain reconciled itself to
planning and the principle of social justice to a considerable
degree. Thus the immediate effect of the war is that the struggle
for victory makes planning a common necessity for all countries
waging the war under modern conditions. The democratic
countries are compelled to plan, and there is no real likelihood
that after the war there will be a return to laissez-faire. In the
same way, Britain's example is apparent in the heavy taxation,
the extension of the social services, insurances against risks,
compensation, etc. In all of them the principle of social justice
and the idea of collective responsibility find institutional expression, and it is likely that not only a return to our pre-war society
with its extreme differences in income and wealth is barred, but
that these reforms will have to continue.

The result of all these changes is that the two main issues of the
pre-war period, planning and social justice, which seemed to make
class wars and revolutions inevitable, are being put into practice,
even though in a modified and moderate form, in the democracies
during the war itself. If in these countries planning is never
going to become totalitarian but is restricted to the control of
the key-positions in the economic life only, and if greater social

justice will never lead to mechanical equalization, this will by many of us be felt as an advantage. For if there is a lesson to be learned from the experiments of the totalitarian states it is this: that ruthless regimentation leads to the enslavement of the citizen, and the mechanistic concept of equality defeats itself, as Russia's example shows, where differentiation of income and many other devices fostering social differentiation were reintroduced.

After the experiences of Russia, Germany and Italy, it seems to me that in this country most of the groups on the Left and the Right find themselves in a less intransigent mood and will be willing to make considerable sacrifices, if reconstruction is possible without class war, revolution and dictatorship. All parties in this country (except a decreasing number of extremists) are united in the realization that the greatest evil is dictatorship.

If this is correct, it means that in the hierarchy of our values a change took place in which greater social justice and a desire for a reasonably planned order remain very important demands, but where the maintenance of freedom, the maintenance of the democratic method of change become even more essential. That means also that the planning of the transition is of even greater significance than the planning of the more distant future, because if, in the period of social reconstruction, freedom and parliamentary control are suppressed, they will probably disappear for good. It is very unlikely that if any class or group once got hold of the powerful machinery of the modern state it would ever give it up spontaneously unless there are democratic devices to check them. The chance that without war or other outside interference a totalitarian regime once established could be overthrown from within through another revolution is very slight.

At a time when the sad results of dictatorial methods become more and more apparent, the Anglo-Saxon democracies are gradually developing as an alternative to the Fascist or Communist order a Third Way, a type of planning which is not totalitarian but is under the control of the community, in which the main forms of freedom are not abolished; the fact is acknowledged that no society is possible without responsible governing groups and that a social remedy against oligarchy is not to replace an old one by a new one but to facilitate the access of the gifted from the lower ranks into the leading positions.

What we have learned from the last decades is that the aim
of social progress is not an imaginary society without a governing
class, but the improvement of the economic, social, political and
educational opportunities for the people to train themselves for
leadership, and an improvement of the method of the selection
of the best in the various fields of social life.

I think I am not in the least blind to the danger-spots and to
the fact that democratic awareness is needed to select from among
the war-time measures those which tend to lead to the Anglo-
Saxon pattern of progressive democracy, and to check those
tendencies which, under the cloak of Democracy and Planning,
would establish a new variety of Fascism. But I do believe that
this country is groping its way to a pattern of society which, once
established, might, with modifications, become the basis of democratic reconstruction all over the world.

It is perhaps not by chance that the craving for social awareness is awakening in this country exactly at a juncture when this
transformation is taking place in reality. And it is hardly mere
curiosity that people, young and old, again and again ask questions about man and his place in a changing society. Unconsciously they feel that all depends on their vigilance and that
we need no longer be afraid to face the social situation as a whole
and to develop our own social philosophy. There is no occasion
for such fears: since we need not be afraid of differences still
existing within our boundaries we can afford to be undogmatic.
The changed situation sees to it that we should become dynamic,
progressive as well as responsible. This new responsibility means
that critical thought will not degenerate into destructive criticism
but will remain conscious of its constructive tasks, caring at
once for change and the maintenance of the basic consensus on
which freedom depends.

To-day all those forces which are determined to fight the forces
of evil and oppression rally round the flag of progressive democracy, which is bound to plan the New Order of Freedom and
Social Justice. In this struggle we shall either be able to produce
the necessary awareness, which turns the tragedy of war into a
creative venture in social reconstruction—or we shall perish.

V

MASS EDUCATION AND GROUP ANALYSIS

I. The Sociological Approach to Education

The recent crisis of Democracy and Liberalism should bring home to those countries which still enjoy freedom some of the deficiencies of their system in the changed conditions of the world. Democracy and freedom can only be saved if we study the gradual transformation of the totalitarian states, not for the sake of imitating their methods but to find out the causes of those structural changes which made dictatorship one of the possible responses to the situation of the modern world. We can only expect to find solutions which accord with our democratic and liberal ideals, if we know why those democratic societies which failed to cope with the new situation were driven to accept the dictatorial system. Although the causes leading to their collapse were very complex and the defects of the modern economic and political order were primarily to blame, no one can deny that the lack of mental resistance played a very large part in this break-down. Not only was the educational system in those countries still unfitted for mass education, but the psychological processes at work outside the school were left without any real social control, and so, of necessity, led to chaos and disintegration.

The great democracies of the West, which because of their greater economic security have not yet passed through an immediate crisis, should not let themselves be deceived by this momentary calm. The very same forces which are transforming the whole structure of society all over the world are at work in them, and we have to ask whether in fact they are better off as regards their educational system. The democratic Governments cannot pride themselves on discovering satisfactory forms of social control to replace a vanishing community culture, or new psychological techniques for dealing with the needs of mass society. A general psychological break-down can only be prevented if we are quick enough to realize the nature of the new situation, and to re-define the aims and means of democratic education accordingly.

This reformation of democratic and liberal aims and methods to fit a new society calls for a sociological approach to education. I shall specify a few of its implications:

(1) Education does not mould man in the abstract, but in and for a given society.

(2) The ultimate educational unit is never the individual but the group, which may vary in size, aim and function. With them will vary the predominant patterns of action to which the individuals in these groups will have to conform.

(3) The educational aims of society cannot be adequately understood as long as they are severed from the situations that each age is called upon to face and from the social order for which they are framed.

(4) Codes and norms are, to the sociologist, not ends in themselves but always the expression of an interplay between individual and group adjustment. The fact that norms are themselves not absolute but change with the changing social order and help to solve the tasks with which society is faced, cannot be seen from the experience of the single individual.[1] To him they seem to be absolute and unalterable decrees, and without this belief in their stability they cannot be made to work. Their true nature and function in society as a form of collective adaptation reveals itself only if we follow their history through many generations, continuously relating them to the changing social background.

(5) These educational aims in their social context are handed down to the new generation together with the prevailing educational techniques. Educational techniques in their turn do not develop in isolation but always as part in the general development of "social techniques." Thus education is rightly understood only if we consider it as one of the techniques of influencing human behaviour and as one means of social control. The slightest change in these more general techniques and controls reacts upon education in the narrow sense, as it is carried out within the walls of the school.

(6) The more we consider education from the point of view of our recent experience, as only one of the many ways of in-

fluencing human behaviour, the more it becomes evident that even the most efficient educational technique is doomed to fail unless it is related to the remaining forms of social control. No educational system is able to maintain emotional stability and mental integrity in the new generation, unless it has a kind of common strategy with the social agencies outside the school. Only through co-operation with them is it possible, particularly in our present age, to hold in check the social influences which otherwise disorganize community life. Only through a co-ordinated attack upon the disorganizing effects of mass society on the mind of the individual can one hope to stem mass psychoses such as developed on the Continent.

This sociological approach to education will probably be resisted by those educationists of the Liberal era to whom the only dignified aim of education seemed to be the development of an independent personality. They thought to have saved the autonomy of the personality by neglecting the analysis of the social context in which man has to act and to survive.

To-day we know that society-blindness, instead of being a virtue, is rather an obsolete method of looking at reality, and that neither the cause of freedom nor the idea of personality is served by blinding oneself to the significance of environmental factors.

In the Victorian age, when a small élite controlled the affairs of democracy, an idealist approach to education disregarding the social content caused no great harm. The social conditions under which these small élites grew up presented enough opportunities for individualization. There was nothing in the surroundings of the privileged few which prevented the growth of an all-round personality in those who had the innate abilities to make the best of these opportunities. Nor did this disregard of the significance of social conditions then lead to visible symptoms of crisis within the masses either, for, in spite of their life of drudgery, mentally they were still sheltered in their community life and the traditional methods of controlling human conduct were fairly efficient, owing to the sluggishness of social development. But this blindness to the social context in which personality is formed passes unpunished only as long as democracy is a democracy of the few. The isolating method of liberal thinking tended to turn every item into an absolute. Thus the aim and technique of education were regarded as entities good or bad in themselves, irrespective of any social background whatever. As soon as the masses become politically active, new forms of education are necessary and the selection and maintenance of the highly individualized standards of the élite become a matter of public concern. At this stage it is no longer possible to confine the problem of education to the school. Education can no longer be considered as an interchange between two individuals, the teacher and the pupil; it can no longer be looked upon as a personal and private relationship, but as a part of the broader context of social processes.

Another unprofitable tendency was to be found in the fact that character was educated for life, and "Life" meant some vague generality: a vacuum in which, according to a mysterious harmony, everything would turn out for the best. To-day we know that this vacuum called "Life" is to a very large extent society, with its changing situations and institutions.

Liberal education, with its lack of insight into the social background, works fairly well when, as in times of prosperity and general expansion, everyone with any strength of character has a good chance of making his way in life. It fails, however, when the general expansion and prosperity cease and the various groups are thrown back upon their own resources; when unemployment and lack of mobility sap the energy of isolated individuals. Ignoring the sociological point of view does not abolish social problems, but leads to complete chaos, marked by the rising influence of those who try to establish order in society, not by scientific guidance, but by dictatorial decree. The sociological shortsightedness of dogmatic thinkers prevents us from realizing that there are methods already at hand within the democratic and liberal framework, which, if adequately developed, could help us to deal with the changing situation. But in order to cope with the new conditions of mass society without paving the way for dictatorship and mechanical conformity, democracy and liberalism must give up their irresponsible optimism and their policy of laissez-faire, and study the principles governing social trends. So we must not think that a knowledge of social conditions prevailing in mass society is equivalent to levelling personality. It is usually possible to break up a Great Society into smaller units, and there to foster those conditions which enhance individual differences between members of a group.

In the same way, the reluctance of the idealist of the previous era to relate norms to the changing historical, social context is bound to pass. A study of the processes which support or destroy the social validity of certain ethical standards does not mean relativism, anarchy and contempt for standards in general, but is only an attempt to find scope for Socratic reflection. Socratic reflection in its original form was the first symptom of democratic change in a society where the best and most alert among the people tried to create a science which should analyse the passing of the old moral codes and mythical explanations in a critical spirit. They hoped to set up rational norms which would be valid for an urban society, and would harmonize with the new habits of thought in a world based on handicraft and commerce.

This system of ethics was the rational way of re-establishing norms in small intellectual groups where custom tended to disappear. When shall we have the courage to admit that our judges, ministers, doctors, teachers, social workers are, in a similar way, continuously faced with the conflicts which confront the individual as he adjusts himself to changing conditions? Now both the person who seeks for advice and the person who is expected to give it are at a loss to know to which norms and ethical standards they should cling. When shall we be willing to admit that, in the chaos in which the old conditions vanish and the new demands are not yet clearly established, systematic discussion of the pros and cons of different standards is badly needed? When shall we understand that the only way to prevent the dictators from forcing new creeds and a new code of ethics down our throats is for us to create a forum in our midst which will give a lead to moral adjustment in a period of rapid transformation? The authority of such a forum would not, of course, be derived from any dictatorial powers, but would reside in the prestige acquired through its being guided by our best minds and its being founded on close contacts with that majority who have to put their theories into practice.

In what follows I wish to draw attention to the emergence of two new problems and to the slow growth of some new psychological techniques which, if further developed, are bound to contribute to the readjustment of individuals and groups in our

society. First, I wish to suggest a possible approach to the
problem of the growth of new democratic standards and their
readjustment to changing social conditions. One of the deepest
sources of the insecurity of democratic culture lies in the fact that
people lose respect for ethical standards in general. The main
reason for this growing contempt is that in a changing society
most of the age-old norms, which were reasonable in their former
context, grow out of date without being abandoned. It is widely
acknowledged that moral commands which can no longer be
fulfilled because they have lost touch with reality, make for an
increase in law-breakers and for a diminishing loyalty to law in
general. The democratic system has not yet set up machinery
which could remove these obsolete rules from our moral code,
as obsolete laws are removed from the statute book. We should
not forget that moral codes, like legal regulations, are devices for
moulding human behaviour. If we have so far been able to do
without institutionalized control in the moral field, this is mainly
because the ethical standards of everyday life have been created
for the most part by trial and error, and transmitted by anonymous
tradition. But trial and error only work as long as social conditions favour unconscious selection: that is, as long as change
takes place so gradually that unworkable norms are sloughed
away in the course of time. This is not what is happening to-day.
The speed of transformation is surely too great to permit unconscious experiment and selection. The individual is lost in an
invisible society, and is too weak to invent new norms for himself.
The result is a moral chaos in which religious standards, family
traditions and neighbourly ethics are losing ground without being
replaced by other principles.

Dictatorial societies arrive at a short-circuit solution. They
simply establish their codes in the spirit of a totalitarian *Gleichschaltung*. In this unscrupulous way they fill a gap which should
be bridged by democratic readjustment, so that both the expert
and the man in the street could work out the new standards
together. But in order to reach this stage, all the competent
agencies in our democratic societies, such as the churches, schools
and social services, must examine our moral standards more
scientifically. They must realize that these standards do not gain
in dignity by pretending they are eternal and unchangeable.
The growth of social work and the social sciences proves that

establishing a moral code is part of the problem of rational adjustment and that the social worker, for instance, constantly interferes with established habits, without really facing the question of standards at all.

Modern sociology and psychology are making progress not only in reforming moral standards, but in finding new methods of readjusting the masses by group analysis. Here we touch upon a problem which was already realized in Greek tragedy, where the meaning of group catharsis was first worked out. Although these experiments are so far isolated and in a very early stage of development (usually even their authors do not know their full significance), I venture to say that we have in them a genuine alternative to the Fascist exploitation of group emotion. We have to break loose from the prejudice that group interaction is capable only of creating mass psychosis, that groups and masses cannot be enlightened, but are bound to be the prey of ideologies. Democracy must learn to use the forces of group interaction in a positive cathartic way.

These two approaches to our problem are obviously not educational in the narrower sense of the word. But it is clear that they are complementary to education, as soon as we realize that all the methods of making adjustment rational (both in individuals and in groups) are only different tools which can be used in the common work of reconstructing human conduct.

II. INDIVIDUAL ADJUSTMENT AND COLLECTIVE DEMANDS

According to the modern approach in psychology and sociology, the real meaning of any human activity can only be found when it is defined in terms of adjustment. Adjustment means that in some way an organism relates its inner and overt behaviour to the requirements of the surroundings.[2] The simplest form of adjustment, that of trial and error, is to be seen in the behaviour of an animal shut up in a cage and trying to escape by running against the bars or by searching in every corner for an exit. When a child learns cleanliness through an inner control over his visceral tensions, we speak of an adjustment to the hygienic demands of his social surroundings. In the same way, if he learns to adjust his emotional tensions to the forms of self-expression customary in his family or his country, we still speak of self-adjustment, although it takes place on a higher level.

Every living being finds itself in a continuous state of adjustment. We tend nevertheless to overlook the fact that our attitudes
are being continuously related to the surrounding world because
under normal and stationary conditions we generally make use of
traditional patterns of behaviour. But traditional patterns of
behaviour like *mores* and conventions are themselves nothing but
the results of former adjustments made by our forefathers. They
survive mainly because they are responses to typical situations
which still arise in our society. As it is only under changing
conditions that we can realize that our behaviour is based upon
adjustment, let us choose as an example a group in rapid transformation.

When one reads about immigrant groups like the Polish
peasants in America, whose conduct is described in a masterly
way by Thomas and Znaniecky,[3] or about the fate of aristocratic refugees in Paris after the Russian revolution, one may
observe certain typical processes and conflicts at work. In
the first stage of its stay in the foreign country, the immigrant
group tends to adjust itself to the new situation as a closed single
unit. Later, some of its members prefer to make their own
adjustment. We speak of collective adjustment, as distinct from
individual adjustment, as long as the group holds together in
some way or other. As long as collective adjustment prevails,
the single member of the group does not act according to his
immediate personal interests but as a member of the whole social
body. It is mainly his feeling of weakness and isolation in hostile
surroundings which makes him subject his personal wishes to the
requirements of the group. At this stage, therefore, mutual help
and spontaneous co-operation is the rule, and each man uses his
talents in the interests of the group. In addition, we find the
whole group identifying themselves with the single member
should he be attacked from without.

This public spirit vanishes when, later, under changing conditions, certain members of the group are offered special opportunities. The younger ones especially, who have learnt the new
language, acquired adequate training, and adapted their habits
of thought to the new mental climate, will have better opportunities than their elders in the choice of a career.

As the objective opportunities change, the subjective reactions
will change also. It is at this stage that a difference between

individual and collective adjustment becomes visible. Whereas
the younger members make their way through individual adjustment, that is to say, by using their special opportunities regardless
of the needs of the group—the older cling more tenaciously to the
collective forms of adjustment. The more hopeless their situation
becomes in the new surroundings, the greater will be their
orthodoxy. They will ascribe a special significance to every detail
of their former aristocratic habits, they will cultivate their class-
consciousness and anti-democratic outlook even more dogmatic-
ally than before. They do so because they feel, even if sub-
consciously, that if the group cohesion on which their fate depends
is to survive, it needs a much stronger emphasis than it did in their
country of origin. From now on their orthodoxy will not only
be a habitual attitude but will become a psychological pressure
upon the young, in an attempt to subordinate to group cohesion
the youthful tendency to individual adjustment.

Here we have an instance in which the problem "Individual
Adjustment and Collective Demands" is illustrated by a single
conflict. One of the essential sources of human conflict is to be
found wherever the optimum of individual adjustment no longer
coincides with the collective demands of the group. Some clash
between the immediate interests of the individual and those of
the group occurs even under stationary conditions in harmonious
community life. Even when the group we are discussing was
living in its country of origin and no signs of any revolutionary
methods were to be seen on the horizon, there was still some
tension present in the day-to-day adjustments. But there was
always the possibility of pointing out to the individual that by
sacrificing some of his immediate personal advantages he would
ultimately stand to gain by sharing in the increased power of the
group. Matters had not yet reached a stage where it was impossible to compromise between individual and community
interests.

To put the problem quite generally: in every case of human
adjustment we are faced with the more or less powerful conflict
between the original impulses of the individual in his search for
maximum satisfaction and self-expression, and the taboos and
prohibitions by which society tries to inhibit them.

Jessie Taft [4] describes how Jack, a little boy, tried to destroy
various objects in her consulting-room and to do all kinds of

forbidden things in order to find out the "limit" the adult would set to his activities. The nature of this "limit" is the problem of the sociologist because the "don'ts" the grown-up inflicts on the child are not simply the expression of his purely personal opinions. These "don'ts" and collective demands are mostly the usual standards of behaviour in a given society, and from his self-adjustments the child gradually learns to find the right compromise between his impulses and the collective demands established by society.

In the last ten to twenty years, which have been marked by the exaggerated individualism of certain groups, there have been many who thought that sociological and psychological readjustment would enable us to live without repressions. They are now beginning to realize that it is impossible to do without them, and that a certain number of inhibitions is inevitable. To us the question is, therefore, not so much whether we can do without conventions and repressions, but whether we can make clear distinctions between taboos, which are nothing but a burden to the mind, and reasonable principles without which a society cannot survive. Thus we are able to determine the principles governing institutions in a successful society and in one which is a failure.

To my mind, there are three main criteria for establishing the distinction between successful and unsuccessful societies:

(a) A successful society will economize as much as possible in the use of prohibitions and repression.

(b) It will distinguish between humane and harmful prohibitions.

(c) Through its institutions it will help the individual to make his adjustment in the best possible way, and will come to the rescue of those who have failed in their readjustments.

Thus our next problem is to know more about the nature of these standards and collective demands, about their social and psychological origin, about their function in past and present-day society. First of all, we have to realize that they are not homogeneous in their nature, and it will be better to deal with them under different headings, according to the contribution they make to the readjustment of groups and individuals.

I shall first mention the rational conventions and taboos which have a definite function in a given social order. Secondly, I shall pass on to those which cause psychological maladjustment because they spring from conflicting institutions. Thirdly, there are standards which were once functional and are now irrational because they have lost all social meaning. Fourthly, we come to other standards which, although they were irrational in themselves, have, by some social process, assumed a real function in contemporary society. Lastly, we shall have to deal with obsolete conventions which have no real function, and thus are simply a psychological burden.

(1) As to the first category, I understand by functional standards those which have a definite function to fulfil without which no society, especially our own, can survive. Thus it would be impossible to permit homicide even if there were a certain aggressiveness inherent in man. In this case the only remedy a society can provide is to find some other outlet or form of sublimation for this drive. In the same way, minor habits like punctuality, discipline, perseverance, thoroughness are to be inculcated into the individual in order to make co-operation possible in our society.

(2) It is a very different matter when we come to those standards which, although they have a function, are in conflict with other standards owing to the lack of co-ordination in our institutions. If the family teaches us neighbourly ethics in which mutual help is a matter of course, while the laws of the market compel us to become self-assertive, the consequence of these conflicting demands will be a kind of neurosis. Thus Karen Horney [5] in her interesting book is right when she says that these types of neuroses are the products of competitive society. These conflicts will never be solved by the individual himself as long as there is no satisfactory co-ordination between social institutions. Yet even here it helps the individual to find a suitable compromise between the conflicting tendencies if he realizes by sociological analysis that the source of the conflict does not rest in him, and that an improvement can only be brought about by a collective effort to co-ordinate our conflicting institutions.

(3) The position is even more complicated if the conflict in the mind of the individual is due to the fact that the standards which serve him as a measuring-rod have no real function in present-day society, although they were quite sensible in the past. The reason why such obsolete standards can survive lies in the fact that man makes most of his adjustments not by genuine

responses but by using cultural patterns of behaviour and traditionally established social standards. Thus, the commands by which he is guided may belong to an earlier stage of society, while the real problems to which he must adjust himself are of recent origin.

Freud has shown that these obsolete demands might be explained in terms of the formation of our Ego-Ideal. The most important elements in the Ego-Ideal are formed in early childhood, and thus very often reflect parental demands. But by the very same mechanism through which we have taken over these demands from our parents, the latter may have got them from their parents, so that they are mostly the reflection of a bygone age. This is the reason why the fundamental set of commands which controls our life, very often lags behind the actual reality to which we have to adjust ourselves.

It is obvious, therefore, that in certain cases a too rigid Ego-Ideal may become, as M. W. Wulff has shown by interesting examples,[6] an impediment to our adjustment to reality. In the case of our emigrant, for instance, the aristocratic traditions had formerly a functional meaning in a society which was based upon the distinction of ranks. But the very same demands become meaningless and intolerable to a person who has to carve out a career in a democratic society. Here rational sociological analysis may be a great asset to the individual, as it explains his difficulties in adjustment and enables him to get rid of standards which have lost their justification.

(4) We are faced with a special difficulty in cases where a superficial analysis would prove some commands to be completely irrational and meaningless whereas a more penetrating analysis might bring out their functional significance. Many of the habits of the old aristocrats, their clinging to all sorts of distinctions and their attributing an even greater importance to ranks and titles than in their country of origin, may seem to a member of the younger generation completely meaningless, as he is adjusting himself to a democratic society in which there is greater equality for all. Were he to look upon these conventions from the standpoint of the older generation he would realize that they are not in the least meaningless. The old conventions have acquired a new function in the new surroundings. They have become a defence mechanism which secretly helps to

maintain cohesion among those who are incapable of individual adjustment.

Thus seemingly irrational attitudes may have a secondary functional meaning when seen from the particular situation of a group. Even here sociological analysis is helpful in finding the right attitudes to these conventions. Those who no longer wish to share the fate of the traditional group will drop them deliberately, while those who value its survival, even under changed conditions, realize their functional meaning.

(5) Finally, I come to a discussion of those standards which are completely irrational, and represent mere ballast in the life of a modern community. No doubt there are many such survivals in our society which arose from the helplessness of earlier social organizations. The elimination of these irrational and meaningless commands becomes legitimate only if we can show the mechanism which produces them. Here I am thinking of those explanations of certain taboos which assert that these prohibitions were due, for instance, to the idiosyncrasies of some powerful personality or to some chance behaviour which was then taken over by the bulk of the people. Prescribed dietary systems or the distinction between clean and unclean foods in their very first origin probably go back to some such personal aversion which spread through suggestion and imitation. In the next generation it may have been a conditioned disgust which was acquired in early childhood. These emotionally fixed habits, then, seem to the person who does not know their origin to be due to some innate horror in man. At this stage, as a rule, some kind of rationalization takes place—an attempt to find a religious or moral justification for the traditional attitudes. If the group mind thinks in terms of magic it may arrive at some totemistic theory of taboo. If the general habits of thought have reached a more utilitarian level, the prohibitions may be justified in terms of their hygienic value. It is obvious, however, that these justifications, although apparently rational, are not in the least reliable as explanations of moral rules.

I may be giving the impression that I only recognize functional and rational standards and that I am overlooking the irrational needs of the human mind and their roots in the unconscious. This, however, is not so. Owing to limitations of space I cannot enter into a discussion of those irrational elements which are completely meaningless, and those which satisfy unconscious needs.[7] At the moment we are impressed by the fact that civilization has placed too great a burden upon the mind of the individual and that the greater part of our neurotic symptoms is the result of superfluous inhibitions. It seems as if certain sexual taboos, certain forms of exaggerated asceticism and restrictions of self-expression are due, not so much to social or psychological needs, as to the fact that society up to the present has been too clumsy a mechanism, wasteful in its working, and so apt to crush the individual psyche. On the other hand, it is possible that the survival of overstrict taboos is due to the authoritarian form of past society which wanted to produce a subservient mind. Perhaps the fostering of guilt and inferiority feeling on a large scale serves to create a subservient citizen, and the taboos laid during childhood on sexual curiosity help to suppress the development of an inquiring mind.

The more Fascism reverts to these obsolete methods of intimidation and to a general tendency to demand unquestioned submission, the more urgent does it become for the psychologist and sociologist in the democratic countries to study methods which are able to replace these brutal forms of social integration by more human forms of education. A well-governed modern society based upon sound institutions can do with less strain and repression in the moral code.

The claim to revise our moral standards is not as new as it would seem. What was the Reformation, and the Puritan movement in particular, other than a thorough-going purge of the magical elements in the Roman Catholic religion in order to achieve a more rational morality? It is a logical continuation of this trend if we to-day plead for collective demands which must be "functional rather than formal, understandable rather than arbitrary, voluntary rather than coercive, and attractive rather than routine." [8]

III. The Problem of Group Analysis

Finally, let me say a few words about the ways in which society can help the individual to make his adjustments. In the early stages the help given to the poor was material. Charity restricted itself to pure externals. It was psychology, especially psycho-analysis, which raised the problem of the subjective side of readjustment. Having admitted this, I do not, however, regard the merely individual help offered by the psycho-analytic method as the last word in social and psychological readjustment. I am rather inclined to think that we are approaching an age in which certain forms of collective adjustment will become as important as individual adjustment. Viewed from this angle, psycho-analysis, which stresses the therapeutic relationship between the single individual and the analyst, seems to be only one of the many possibilities of psychological treatment. The disadvantage of the purely individual approach is that the patient is severed from his social background, and treated in the consulting-room, which is not part of his normal surroundings. The analyst has to rely mainly on the results of introspection, and the form of self-adjustment which results is not part and parcel of the patient's daily life. Further, the psycho-analytic approach does not take adequate account of the whole social and cultural background, which is very often finally responsible for the neurotic symptoms.

This purely individualist approach is, indeed, a symptom of the Liberal age, and shares both its advantages and its one-sidedness. As we have seen, the Liberal method of dealing with the problems of man and society was always to tear the individual from his social setting. Thus, in considering the cause and the cure of psychological maladjustments, especially neurosis, it was inclined to overlook the working of the broader social forces. Although we realize the limitations of psycho-analysis, that does not mean that we are opposed to it. On the contrary, the therapeutic relationship between two individuals is often irreplaceable. However, we want to stress the fact that psycho-analytic readjustment does not cover the whole field. Side by side with it there are other forms which are about to be tried out. I have called these collective forms of readjustment, socio-analysis or group analysis. Socio-analysis refers the individual case, not only to the family constellation, but to the whole configuration of social institutions. At the same time, socio-analysis makes more conscious use of group interaction. Such an approach will gradually lead to a control of the immediate and more distant surroundings and will pay equal attention to the cultural and material elements in them. As such trends never appear in isolation but always simultaneously, I should like to draw the attention to some of these attempts, which at the moment are still in an experimental stage. Perhaps it is not too presumptuous to predict that society, which is coming to rely more and more on scientific guidance, will at some future date make use of them.

(1) The first of these experiments in collective readjustment is but a modification of the psycho-analytic technique, applied in certain cases to smaller groups. These experiments were first carried out in the wards of a mental home where it was necessary to find a technique for the intramural treatment of a great number of patients by a relatively small staff. Instead of analysing individuals, an attempt was made to bring about the analytic situation in small groups. The analyst started by discussing different types of psychological maladjustment. The more he worked on these lines the more obvious it became that this discussion had a releasing effect. One has only to remember the eagerness with which patients in small groups discuss their ailments to see the possibilities. According to these experiments, it depends mainly on the analyst's ability whether he makes good use of this emotional tension in the group and whether he is able to guide it into therapeutic channels. Another reason why group discussion had a releasing effect was that it helped some of the patients to establish contact with the analyst, and this gradually developed into a kind of transference. Louis Wender,[9] some years ago, read a paper before the New York Neurological Society describing these experiments in some detail, and he observed, among other things, that the resistance of the patients is sometimes weaker than in individual analysis. The reason seems to be that the neurotic symptoms and the different forms of maladjustment in these cases are described without reference to special individuals. The patient thus learns to recognize his symptoms in other people, and it is only later that he connects them with himself.

Nothing could be worse than to regard this experiment as a substitute for psycho-analysis, or to judge it by the psycho-analytic criteria. It is something entirely different, and it is not so much a radical cure in difficult cases as an attempt to set a mechanism in motion by giving it a push. One will only find the right approach to this experiment and to those which follow if one realizes how great is the range of those as yet unexplored techniques which try to use group influence in its positive aspects.

Let us refer to Thrasher's [10] observation on gang behaviour. According to him, it is impossible to change a young boy who is a member of a gang by teaching and admonition—that is to say, by means of an individual approach. But it is possible to achieve some success in readjustment by taking him as a member of his gang, and by giving the gang a new and socially useful task. Then the youngster will be changed not as an individual but as a member of a gang, and in this way the unexplored forces of group interaction will become a powerful means of re-education.

(2) Aichhorn's [11] method represents another form of group readjustment. In his child guidance work, before meeting the child himself he tries to come into contact with the parents in order to detect, by watching their behaviour, the possible sources of the neurotic symptoms in the child. In the same way, his treatment and guidance is not so much centred on the individual as on the neurotic constellation in the family, and he tries to bring the force of transference to bear upon the parents as well as the child. Of course, Aichhorn does not think that this method will replace individual analysis, which must be used if it is needed, but only that there are a great many cases in which the readjustment of the emotional constellation in the family is the right method. This obviously leads to a control of the surroundings, which, in its definition of "milieu," include not only the material facts, but also the emotional and intellectual setting.

(3) Once one realizes that neurotics can be helped in their readjustment by controlling the tensions which arise in their surroundings, one must admit that it is not only the immediate surroundings like the family, the neighbourhood or the professional background which are responsible for psychological pressure. The mental climate of a given society as a whole may be the source of unbearable tensions in the individual. Here I have to draw the attention of the reader to that new branch of knowledge which is called the analysis of ideologies. By ideologies we understand those interpretations of situations which are not the outcome of concrete experiences but are a kind of distorted knowledge of them, and which serve to cover up the real situation and work upon the individual like a compulsion. The existence of ideologies was first noticed in the political sphere.[12] If one discusses problems with fanatical Communists, Fascists, or even democrats, one suddenly feels that the individual does not adopt

an empirical attitude, but rather defends his views in a way which can only be called obsessional thinking.

But ideologies are not only confined to politics. There is practically no sphere of life, as Schilder [13] has shown, which is not smothered in ideologies. Take, for instance, the facts concerning love, sex, masculinity or femininity, or questions of social advancement and success [14] or our traditional attitudes to money. Either they must not be discussed in public or, if admitted at all, they are dressed up in conventional prejudices. We know that whenever a subject is excluded from public discussion it will become a source of neurotic symptoms or stunted development.

As most of these ideologies are not invented by the individual but are instilled into him by the community, and as they are usually deeply rooted in the unconscious, it is very difficult to remove them. Observations show that strong defence mechanisms are at work, which are all the more dangerous as these forms of collective fear, guilt and hatred not only hinder understanding between groups but cause neurotic symptoms in the individual. It gradually becomes obvious to most of us that these symptoms cannot be successfully removed by curing the individual alone or by merely reconditioning small groups like the family or the neighbourhood. Unless a large-scale attack is made on the defence mechanisms by education, propaganda and social work, the poisoned mental atmosphere of the whole nation will always be stronger than the readjusted individual or the smaller group. Until this is done, the obsessional forms of public ideologies will act as a stumbling-block to education and will frustrate the work of personal enlightenment. A new form of teaching will generally be necessary. Before any constructive work is possible the defence mechanisms must be broken down. This is done by laying bare the hidden springs of ideologies and then showing that they are connected with unconscious motives or latent interests. One must draw attention to the fact that we are all subjected to some of these mechanisms, and that they are the greatest obstacle to dealing rationally with our problems. Only when the individual is ready for introspection can one proceed to logical argument, showing that these ideologies are inconsistent or are concealing under empty symbols just those problems which the individual does not want to face. In seminary work and in lectures one very often has the impression that this kind of ideological analysis of social and psychological facts not only broadens the outlook but gradually changes the attitude of the audience and brings about a kind of catharsis. Recently the psychiatrist Schilder [15] tried to apply the method of ideological analysis and found it very helpful both as a preparation for psycho-analytic treatment and in group readjustment. Once more it would be erroneous to claim that this method is a substitute for psycho-analysis. It fulfils quite a different function in the therapeutic adjustment. In the first place, it makes a more conscious use of the forces of social stimulation for improving the individual than has hitherto been customary. Thus the new form of analysis makes an immediate appeal to the whole group, that is to say, to a group of people in a special setting in which the very same force, wrongly guided, produced ideologies and mental distortions. By the way, I do not think that there is a mystical entity known as the "group mind." But there are, no doubt, evils which arise and can only be cured in configurations which we call social, where group interaction is at work, and where a simultaneous attack on the many facilitates the removal of resistance. I am sure every one of us has, at some time or other, had similar experiences of collective release either through attending well-directed meetings on sexual reform or other methods of public enlightenment. As an anonymous member of the audience it was easier for us to get rid of certain prejudices which were a burden to the mind than if we had had to discuss them personally. Moreover, it has rightly been said that in such cases the individual's feeling of isolation suddenly ceases when he notices that he is not the only person who is secretly tormented by feelings of guilt, and that he shares them with the majority of his fellows.

In the light of these experiences, we suddenly regard the whole development of recent centuries quite differently. The whole process, starting with the seventeenth and eighteenth centuries and known as the age of enlightenment, is not only a new trend of ideas but a continuous series of attempts at a new kind of group analysis. We must not blame these early pioneers for trying to remove psychological stumbling-blocks by reason. I would stress the healing power of reason even over collective action. I do so the more consciously as it seems to be the fashion to believe that recent events in Germany and elsewhere have

proved that the masses are capable only of irrational attitudes
and emotional epidemics. I do not deny the possibility of ex-
ploiting mass emotion in that way. But before I agree with
such a general contempt for the masses I first suggest a thorough
study of the cases, both in history and contemporary society, in
which a skilful handling of their problems brought about enlightenment and group catharsis. We very often see the masses
fighting for enlightened values, and we all know many examples
of their craving for education. Perhaps the evil does not rest
with the people themselves but with the lack of goodwill among
the élite which might have helped them, and with our ignorance
of the possible techniques of approach and of their different
reactions on the individual. The exclusive concentration upon
the individual leads to a complete neglect of the different settings
in which people live. Just as a child behaves differently when
he is in a family, in a play-room, in a gang, so it is found that
different types of institutions react very distinctly upon the
behaviour and self-expression of the individual.

(4) Not only should we study by experiment how to make
the best use of the forces of mass interaction, but we should take
into account another trend in the development of sociological
thought. The clear distinction between group and crowd shows
that it was a great mistake of certain psychologists, such as Le
Bon and his followers, to cast suspicion at every association of
the many by calling it a crowd or mass. This corresponds to
the attitude of the former élite which led them to give up their
belief in modern society just because new groups claimed entrance
to civilization. The most interesting representative of this kind
of attitude is Ortega y Gasset's *The Revolt of the Masses*,[16] which,
although very stimulating, suffers from the same limitation. By
identifying the increasing numbers in society with the mass these
thinkers prevent a conscientious distinction between the different
possibilities of the different forms of group integration. Not
every grouping of the many is a mass or crowd. It is important
to notice at this point that groups with definite functions and
inner articulation do not lower but raise the mental level of their
members, whereas the disintegration of personality generally
corresponds to disintegrations in society.

The task of the future is, therefore, clearly to distinguish
between the innumerable forms of group integration, and to know

xactly how they react upon the minds of their members. Valu-
ble experiments have been made in America, in Russia, and
ther countries, which show, for instance, how working in a
roup reacts upon the achievement of the individual.[17]

In this context the school-class itself has been studied as a
ocial group with special possibilities.[18] Then the significance
f work must be realized. By creating co-operation, distributing
isks and responsibilities, it is a primary agency in developing
ersonality within the social pattern. The novelty of the *Arbeits-
chule* [19] lies in its conscious use of group work to stimulate the
rowth of personality. Besides, work-play and games have not
nly an educational value but a specific cathartic power. It was
ightly said [20] that they have much the same effect as dreams,
ecause they provide an outlet for repressed instincts and dis-
ociated ideas. Games have, further, the advantage of being co-
perative or individualistic in varying degrees. Thus it has been
bserved that the Greek games were pre-eminently individualistic,
hereas the English national games were from the very beginning
o-operative, strengthening community spirit.[21] Shall we add
hat the Fascist conception of games introduces the militaristic
attern?

Thus, the results both of theoretical analyses and empirical
bservations show that the first result of the transformation of
norganized masses into institutionalized groups is the creation
f "institutional behaviour" in the individual.[22] But this is only
he first step. Great divergences arise owing to different functions
he groups have to fulfil. These react upon their articulation,
nd this in its turn is immediately reflected in the different mental
evels and in the reactions of the individuals concerned.[23] Lastly,
here is not only a difference between mass and group; there is
 corresponding difference between mass- and group-leader.[24]
The great psychological and sociological problem in the future
s, therefore, how to organize inarticulate masses and crowds
nto various forms of group, each with a different educational
nfluence in forming personality.

Let us consider in this connection the task of education and
f the new social services. The social worker, for instance, is in
 very favourable position with regard to his patient. He does
ot meet him only in an office or consulting-room but has access
o the whole family and an insight into the whole social setting.

D*

Moreover, he is a "liaison officer" between the actual situation to be faced in society and our general social policy. He can steer both the super ego of the individual and the collective trend of public opinion. In a word, he can co-ordinate social change in terms of individual adjustment and of collective demands.

As we have seen, the drawback to the psycho-analytic approach arises from the fact that it has access only to the individual self. It is thus unable to cope with the paradox of the vicious circle. On the one hand, individuals are determined by society and on the other, society is made up of individuals. For education and social work the solution lies in co-ordinating the attack on individuals and on the community.

Although these new trends and the psychological techniques mentioned in this paper still are in their infancy, it is very probable that they will develop, so that the new collective demands will gradually be controlled by cautious forethought and experiment. Just as rational legal regulation grew out of *mores* and customary law, so the taboos which regulate our habits will have to stand the test of scientific probing.

By accumulating many concrete experiences we shall know empirically how these standards work in different situations, and how far individual adjustment clashes with existing collective demands. A sound knowledge of the obstacles to individual adjustment and of the collective demands which are based upon the functional needs of society as a whole, will gradually lead us to redraft our moral codes. The educationist and the representatives of the new social services have the special opportunity of standing at the cross-roads where they can gain insight both into the working of the individual psyche and of society. They, more than others, have the power to link up the regeneration of man with the regeneration of society.

VI

NAZI GROUP STRATEGY

Hitler has invented a new method which could be called Nazi group strategy. The main point about Hitler's psychological strategy is that he never approaches the individual as person but always as a member of a social group. What Hitler does instinctively is in keeping with discoveries of modern sociology, namely, that man is most easily influenced through his group ties. What is even more important, his reactions vary according to the particular group. Man behaves differently in the family, in the club, in the army, in business life, or as a citizen at large. The great Duke of Marlborough was head of the army, yet at home he was under the thumb of his wife. Each group seems to have its own traditions, its own prohibitions, its own forms of self-expression, and as long as these groups are intact, they support and guide the behaviour of their members.

I. SYSTEMATIC DISORGANIZATION OF SOCIETY [1]

Hitler instinctively knows that as long as people are sheltered in their own social groups, they are immune from his influence. The hidden device of Hitler's strategy is, therefore, to break the resistance of the individual mind by disorganizing the groups to which those individuals belong. He knows that a man without group ties is like a crab without its shell. This disorganization, like his blitz tactics in war, must be both rapid and violent. But even so, its effect will be lasting only if he succeeds in building up immediately new groups which will promote the kind of behaviour approved by his own party.

Thus there are two main stages in Hitler's group strategy: breaking down the traditional groups of civilized society and a rapid rebuilding on the basis of an entirely new group pattern. In the work of disintegration, he can, of course, rely to a large extent on the planlessness of our economic life. For example, lack of planning is responsible for that most demoralizing of conditions, permanent unemployment. But where this spontaneous disintegration has not proceeded far enough to suit Hitler's purposes, he applies his own methods. He has different methods for dealing with the family, the church, political parties and nations. The elements of this technique he learned from the Communists, but the details of it he elaborated in his own struggle in the political jungle of Germany of the nineteen-twenties. He learned how to break up mass meetings, to demoralize followers of other parties to appear to co-operate with rival groups and then, when the time was ripe, to bring about their downfall. All he has done recently is to transfer this group strategy to the realm of foreign policy.

Take the case of nations. Here his first rule seems to be never to use force until he has exhausted the possibilities of demoralization. He knows that groups, especially whole nations, with a sound group life and intact morale react to open threats and direct attack with defiance. They become even more united than before. This healthy group life is the secret of Britain's unbreakable resistance, and accounts for Hitler's hesitation in attacking her.

When he is able to find Quislings within the groups, he use the technique of group penetration. He sends emissaries a tourists and in other disguises to win over to his side both the opponents of the existing régime and those who are misfits and social failures. Having organized the mass agents of an underground movement, he tries to isolate the nation from the outside world. Outflanking, encirclement and complete isolation are the main stages in that process. By this time the victim is entirely at his mercy. But Hitler still avoids direct attack and prefers the method of complete demoralization from within. In the prevailing tension rumours are spread, fears created, rival groups played off against each other, and finally the well-known Nazi mixture of threats and promises is administered. These are the methods he used in Austria, Czechoslovakia, Rumania, Bulgaria and other countries. The secret documents captured in the Lofoten raid in Norway clearly show how systematic these methods are. Nazi army instructions anticipated every possible source of resistance and indicated the counter-measures.

II. Effect on the Individual

At this stage the demoralization and breaking up of social groups begins to take effect on the individual. And what is more on vast numbers of individuals simultaneously. The psychological explanation of this fact is simply this: man left to himself cannot offer resistance. Since his group ties give him support, security and recognition, to say nothing of valuable bonds of friendship and trust, the breaking of these ties renders him helpless. He behaves like a child who has lost his way or lost the person he loves, and consequently feels insecure, ready to cling to anyone who comes along.

In addition to all this, modern methods of total warfare or total propaganda give the individual no time to recover, no chance to rally around a leader and to take the risk of resisting. In small nations particularly, there is let loose overnight almost complete social chaos and a state of lawlessness. This has an important bearing on the individual's subsequent behaviour. The fact is that disintegration of the group tends to be followed by a break-down of the moral conscience in the individual. He is tempted to pursue some such train of thought as this: "After all, every-thing I have believed so far may have been wrong. It may be that life is nothing but a struggle for survival and supremacy. The choice before me is either to become a martyr or to join the new order. Perhaps I might become a prominent member of it. Besides, if I do not join to-day, to-morrow may be too late." It is in this mood that people permit themselves to swallow state-ments such as that made by the Nazi Minister of Justice. He said this: "Formerly we were in the habit of saying, 'Is this right or wrong?' To-day we must put the question thus: 'What would the Führer say?'" It is to this kind of thinking that Hitler's cynical opportunism appeals, and to which his gospel of violence and the law of the mighty is addressed.

One has often emphasized the part played by fear, hatred, insecurity and suspicion in the Nazi régime. I, for my part, would like to add to this catalogue the element of despair. At the bottom of all Nazi reactions lies despair. Their world is one in which everyone feels betrayed, isolated, in which no one any longer trusts his neighbour.

III. The "New Order"

Having successfully reduced the community to panic and despair, Hitler then initiates the second movement of his strategy. He attempts to reconstruct a new order along two distinct lines. One is calculated to enslave the masses, the other to entrench his

leadership and the terrorism of his Party. For the first purpos
he adopts a military organization based on the Prussian model
He applies it to everything, to the organization of youth, to th
organization of industry, labour and of opinion. Here again h
exploits fear, hatred and terrorism. For it is much easier to fin
an outlet for the hostile feeling of groups than it is to harness thei
constructive energies. Hence the use made of "races" an
individuals as scapegoats. The alleged inferiority and devilry c
Jews are made an excuse for spitting in their faces, beating ther
up or murdering them in cold blood. The scapegoat system no
only helps to relieve the community of guilt feeling, but prevent
hostility being turned against the leader when dissatisfaction i
aroused. Of course, the scapegoat need not necessarily be a hom
product. The leaders of all countries who oppose Nazism can b
pointed out as targets for hostility instead of Hitler. And so w
find him accusing Mr. Churchill of every sin in his own calendar

IV. Making the New Leaders

But military organization and suppression alone would not b
enough. Hitler knows that if his type of society is to survive, i
needs something more dynamic than regimentation. So h
develops centres of emotional fermentation of which the gangs o
storm-troopers are the model. These derive directly from post-wa
military bands which from the very beginning endangered anc
tried to dissolve civil society. But their organization and mentalit
owed also a great deal to the early gangs of the German Youtl
movement at its *Wandervogel* stage. The secret aim of these group
is to perpetuate the psychological attitude of adolescence. Thi
accounts for much that seems peculiar in the Nazi State. Just a
it is possible to make family influence so strong that the mentalit
of its members remains retarded and juvenile, so it is possible b
using group devices to maintain and spread an immature anc
unbridled juvenility in society at large. In the Führer-school
where they train for leadership, everything is done to produce
strange blend of infantile emotionalism and blind submission
The Nazis know that their type of leader flourishes only in gang
like groups. It is mainly to these audiences with an artificiall
retarded emotional development that Hitler's hysterical scream
ings appeal. When Churchill says: "I have nothing to offe
but blood, tears, toil and sweat," he appeals to nations of adults

The main purpose of this analysis is to draw attention to the need for developing a counter-strategy. In particular, the democracies must do everything in their power to remedy the disintegrating effects of industrial civilization on our family and community life. But they must do more than protect themselves from contagion. The really promising thing in the new group method is that it can be used for constructive purposes. Hitler has only misused and distorted a so-far neglected potentiality: the creative powers of group existence. The time for the better utilization of group methods will come when we are faced with the problem of reorganizing the world on new lines and with the task of reconditioning the Nazi Mind.

VII

TOWARDS A NEW SOCIAL PHILOSOPHY

A CHALLENGE TO CHRISTIAN THINKERS BY A SOCIOLOGIST *

PART I. CHRISTIANITY IN THE AGE OF PLANNING

(1) *Christianity at the Cross-roads.   Will it associate itself with the Masses or side with Ruling Minorities?*

With the coming of the Renaissance and Liberalism, Christianity failed to remain the basic ferment and integrating force in social life.   The main consequences of this failure deserve special attention.

(*a*) The spiritualization and regulation of human affairs, public and private, has gradually been left to the competing institutions in society—to family, community, business, trade unions, parties, army, public opinion and its exponents, press, wireless, cinema, associations, age groups, groups of intelligentsia, clubs, etc.   At the beginning of the new era, this secularization of the forces in society produced a stimulating variety of human experience, brought the idea of spontaneity and experimentalism home to the members of the community, and led to a process of constant re-valuation.   But in its final outcome this great variety of experience, and the fact that the competing value systems cancelled each other out, led to the neutralization of values in

---

* This chapter was written for a group of friends, Christian thinkers.   Apart from some alterations and further clarification, the argument has been left in its original form in order to serve its original purpose of stimulating thought rather than pretending to give final solutions to the questions raised.

The group, consisting of theologians, clergymen, academic teachers, Civil Servants, writers, etc., used to meet four times a year for a week-end with the avowed purpose of understanding recent changes in society in their relevance for Christianity.   Several years ago, the author was invited to join the group as a sociologist, and in this capacity he wrote the present statement.   In order to preclude any misunderstanding, and as personal feelings are more easily roused in the sphere of religion than perhaps in any other, he wishes to emphasize that he speaks as a sociologist, and as a sociologist only.   The question put to the sociologist can only concern the relationship to, and the function in, society which religion has as one among other spiritual phenomena in the social process.   Whatever this approach may yield, it does not judge the intrinsic values of Christianity and Christian Ethics.

The author also wishes to express his gratitude to all those members of the group who have greatly helped him in a continual give-and-take in the formulation of these problems.

100

general. This is one of the reasons why liberal society at its present stage is handicapped in resisting the spiritual and political challenge coming from the totalitarian states.

(*b*) Of course the withdrawal of the Christian Churches from the main zones of social life was not complete: wherever they maintained their hold on tradition and influenced the ways of life, their impact was very considerable. But wherever they lost touch with the concrete, topical issues of social life, this immediately reacted upon them by increasing formalism and reducing religion to an affair of attending Sunday sermons. This applies less to this country than to the Continent, but the general trend seems to be the same.

(*c*) To this loss of a foothold in society at large by the Churches very often corresponded a readiness on the part of their leaders to co-operate with the ruling classes and to identify themselves with their vested interests both in a spiritual and in a material sense. Still even here there seems to exist an important difference between the basic situation on the Continent and in England. As the emergence of Capitalism and the corresponding social revolutions occurred at a very early stage in England, when religion was still alive and permeated society as a whole, both the conservative and the progressive forces developed their philosophies within the set framework of religion. For that reason it is in this country still possible to be progressive and religious at the same time, whereas on the Continent, where the social antagonisms were formulated before and during the French Revolution, the dominant polarity (with some exceptions) is to be either progressive and an atheist and rationalist, or conservative and very likely religious.

(*d*) This close association between Conservatism, or even Reaction, and the Church contributed a great deal in its turn to the prevailing distrust felt by the public regarding most of the proposals coming from the Church to give a lead to social change and organization.

(2) *Why the Liberal Era could do without Religion. The Need for Spiritual Integration in a Planned Society*

A liberal and competitive economy and its society can function quite well with neutralized values as long as there is no threat from within or without which makes a basic consensus imperative.

This is obviously the case when totalitarian states attack our societies. But not only this negative instance, the assault from outside, makes it a social necessity to have society integrated on those deep levels on which religion integrated pre-industrial societies; the need for planning within our own societies calls for a similar integrating bond. It is not a matter of chance that both Communism and Fascism try to develop and superimpose a pseudo-religious integration in order to create a psychological and sociological background for planning.

It is one of the most important tasks of the sociologist to point out those new functions in the system of planning which make that basic integration necessary, with which a liberal society could dispense. I shall only enumerate some of these functions.

(a) Planned democratic society needs a new type of party system, in which the right to criticize is as strongly developed as the duty to be responsible to the whole. That means that the liberal education for intelligent partisanship, which is mainly defending the interests of your faction and party and leaves the final integration to a large extent to the natural harmony of interests, must gradually be replaced by a new education for responsible criticism, wherein consciousness of the whole is at least as important as awareness of your own interests. In a planned society it is not the natural interplay of interests which gradually leads to a total scheme of action, but a plan intelligently conceived and accepted by all parties. It is obvious that such a new morality can only be achieved if the deepest sources of human regeneration assist the rebirth of society.

(b) As I pointed out, formerly there was need for short-term decisions only. The more matters become interdependent in planned society, the more the long-range consequences of a decision become relevant. The conflict between short-term interests and long-range responsibilities becomes a matter of daily deliberation. Only a generation which has been educated through religion, or at least on the religious level, to discriminate between immediate advantage and the lasting issues of life will be capable of accepting the sacrifice which a properly planned democratic order must continually demand from every single group and individual in the interests of the whole.

(c) Planned society needs a unifying purpose. This can be

achieved either by the extermination or internment of those who do not agree, or by a spiritual integration of the members of society.

This statement requires some further qualification. One could argue that, as far as economic planning is concerned, there is no need for an all-embracing purpose, for a unifying philosophical outlook. The superimposing of the latter is mostly due to the exaggerated zeal of intellectual groups in totalitarian states, who wish to dominate other people. From the limited point of view of economic planning, it is only necessary to agree on economic issues, as, e.g., how much should be produced, what should be produced, how much should be accumulated, how much immediately consumed. Even in the case of total economic planning it is not necessary to plan spiritual issues, just as it is sufficient to co-ordinate the time-tables of the different railway lines without controlling the topics of conversation inside the carriages. But this is exactly what the totalitarian systems demand from their citizens, namely, not only to accept guidance in matters of organization but to allow their whole intellectual outlook and emotional life to be moulded by the central authority. It is possible to a large extent to isolate economic issues from the spiritual ones, and every form of planning for freedom will try to confine the powers of the planner in the economic field to that minimum of interference which is wanted in order to avoid chaos (to avoid, for instance, the development of the trade cycle). Yet, even so, there will be economic regulations which through their implications or immediate consequences will affect spheres of human life other than economics.

Most of the relevant economic decisions affect some groups and classes favourably and others unfavourably. The planner may be careful only to decide the crucial issues from the centre and to allow the maximum of freedom to individual initiative in the elaboration of the plan in the sphere of production and to personal choice in the sphere of consumption; yet his decisions will inevitably prejudice many decisions in the wider life of the community. It will, for instance, somehow be settled in advance at what speed we shall spend or invest, where we shall invest, and, by implication, decisions will be taken as to how much should be spent on social services, religion, education, art, science and so forth.

It would, however, be a great mistake to regard this sort of interference as an entirely novel development. After all, every democratic system has to deal with such issues in its budget and has to develop methods of reaching agreement on controversial issues, even if they affect the differing interests or divergent creeds prevailing in the community. The novelty in a planned system is that such agreements will be reached not by stages only, bit by bit, through compromise on partial issues, but through agreement on a coherent plan founded on consistent principles, a plan which will undertake to determine the general direction of the development for five or ten years to come.

There is yet another reason why the unifying purpose in a planned society is more relevant than in a laissez-faire system. There are issues on which we must agree, not because they are economic in nature or are affected by steps taken in the economic field, but because the chaos of the last twenty years has revealed that not only economic laissez-faire produced structural maladjustment, e.g. mass unemployment, but that nearly every other sphere of social life has a chaos of its own. Therefore, it is not sufficient merely to say with the planning-minded economists, "Let us get things right in the economic sphere and the remainder of the life of society will then take care of itself." It would be very desirable if that were true and everything beyond economics were arranged by the spontaneous self-regulating powers of group life. It certainly would be more pleasant to live in a world where there was no need for interference whatsoever with the life of the spirit. Unfortunately, the planning-minded economist's generosity and laissez-faire attitude in fields other than economics is really due to his lack of knowledge of those other fields, and to his inability to realize that the method of spontaneous adjustment has failed in them too.

Sociological analysis reveals that what we call "the moral crisis" or the crisis in valuations [1] does not simply arise from wickedness in modern man but to a considerable extent is due to the failure of Great Society to re-establish on a larger scale the methods of value adjustment, value assimilation, value reconciliation and value standardization which were always active in small communities, and which, owing to the limited size of those communities, could do their work spontaneously. In the same way, simpler societies could do without a consistent and closely argued educational policy, because their traditions contain co-ordinating influences which work unconsciously. Under the changed conditions of Great Society, however, lack of conscious direction of educational issues leads to what has been called "Education for Chaos." Or to mention another instance: Non-interference with the press led to freedom of opinion as long as little capital was needed, and one could always found a new paper if the existing ones failed to tell the truth. In an age of large industrial combines, lack of community control places the power to shape public opinion into the hands of a few great monopolists.

It is always the same story: laissez-faire, free competition, free adjustment were efficient as long as small self-adjusting units governed the field—whereas the same laissez-faire leads to monopolies, maladjustment of various types and in all fields of social life as soon as the units grow in size and if there is nobody to watch the symptoms of disorganization and to check the cumulative effects of unco-ordinated growth. Under these conditions freedom will not consist in non-interference, but in a control which gives guidance in a democratically agreed direction. What we have learned is that with the advent of Great Society the habit of letting things take their own course does not represent the principle of real freedom, but simply surrenders the cultural inheritance to a few Capitalist concerns, which reflect only too often the lowest common denominator of democratic culture, such as Hollywood, privately owned radio stations and the press. At the present stage of development, Freedom can only be achieved if its conditions are organized according to the democratically agreed wishes of the community. But the latter can prevail only if the community has a vision of aims to be achieved and a knowledge of the means by which they can be achieved. Although even here Planning for Freedom will consist in avoiding interference where it is avoidable there will still be need for agreement where direction is lacking. This guidance can only be given if the integration of the community goes much deeper than is the case at this moment when the forces of disintegration have done their best to undermine tacit consensus and to over-emphasize differences existing in our midst.

(d) Another reason why religious and religion-like movements develop in the present age is that the transition from a laissez-faire liberal system to one utterly different, a planned society, can only occur if the attitudes of men, their whole set of valuations change in a relatively short time. Now, it is a psychological experience that such a sudden change of habits can only take place if enthusiasm or an emotionalization of the new issues accompanies it, and the latter occurs only when the crucial issues of life can be re-defined and gain new significance. This re-definition of the issues in our world does not occur in a piece-meal fashion, and this general re-valuation can only happen if each new objective is part of a new world view and a new way of life. It is this entirely new enthusiasm which lends significance to every individual's life and every activity in it. I pointed out the need and scope for such new experiences on the religious level in order to show where modern society is open to religion; it is a matter of human quality whether genuine religious experiences will emerge, or pseudo-religious movements will be produced as a substitute, as has happened in the totalitarian states. Of course, this complete penetration of life by religion will only occur if those who represent Christian tradition are once more able to go back to the genuine sources of religious experience and do not think that the habitual and institutional forms of religion will suffice for the reconstruction of man and society. Only if the rebirth of religion, both in terms of a popular movement and of regenerated leadership, coincides with the forthcoming social transformation can it happen that the new democratic order of this country will be Christian.

(3) *Catholicism, Protestantism and the Planned Democratic Order*

In this new penetration of Christianity, Catholicism and Protestantism have a different position. Catholicism has the advantage of having in many aspects maintained the pre-Capitalist and pre-individualist interpretation of Christianity. In many ways it may be easier for this tradition to understand the needs of a social order beyond individualism. Protestantism, in its genuine forms, is handicapped in that it itself helped to produce the modern individualist mind and to develop those psychological attitudes which keep the system of Capitalism, competition and free enterprise going. On the other hand, the advantage of Protestantism is that it is nearer to modern man's predicament, and thus might genuinely produce out of the existing state of mind those transformations which will represent adequate solutions for our age. Again, Catholicism, through its Thomistic traditions, very early developed a kind of sociology which was accustomed to deal with social institutions in terms of functions. This produced an attitude of mind in which it is a matter of course to look at institutions not as they present themselves to personal experience and in the individual's private life, but in terms of the objective functions which these institutions fulfil in the life of society as a whole. Protestantism, laying all emphasis on the Augustinian tradition of inner experience, tends to become vague about the social implications of human activities. Another asset of Catholicism is its courage to associate religious experience, wherever possible, with strict rationality and responsible thought. In this, it is a great counterpoise to the woolliness of unbridled irrationality of modern movements. This does not mean that emotions and irrationalism do not represent real power in human life, but only that without an ordered life, the spiritualization and rationality which go with it they are destructive and self-defeating.

On the other hand, the danger of this Catholic sociology is that it leads to mediaevalism, to a kind of reapplication of mediaeval patterns of social organization to large-scale society. There is a profound difference between the community spirit in a pre-individualist age and the new forms of collectivism and integration following the breakdown of Liberalism. The first corresponded to an agricultural society with small cities, where handicraft prevailed: the latter will have to solve the problems of a Great Society with a world economy, in an age of large-scale industrial and social techniques. This at once raises the question of how far the return to a guild system (e.g. "Corporativism") is an adequate solution. So far, it seems to have served as a façade to the Fascist type of minority rule. On the other hand, this should not make us blind to the possible merits of syndicalist solutions. It may be that they went wrong in the existing totalitarian experiments but have significance and merits to be used in our social reconstruction.

The genuine contribution of Protestantism is bound to come from its emphasis on the freedom of the individual, its self-determination, its emphasis on voluntary co-operation, self-help and mutual aid. These will always be the great antitheses to the coming forms of authoritarianism, centralization and organ-

ization from above. It would be misleading to interpret our
appreciation of the significance of systematic thought in Thomism
as an attempt to ignore the contribution Protestantism has made
to the growth of modern rationalism. Just the opposite is true.
Max Weber's [2] historical investigations have shown how the
spirit of modern Capitalism—foresight, calculation, systematiza-
tion of life—developed as an answer to the challenge of the
Calvinist doctrine of predestination. Let us add to this that the
attempt to replace the Church-dictated interpretation of the
world by sects and individuals represents a continuous effort to
reinterpret the world in terms of one's own peculiar experiences.
Those reinterpretations equally make use of rational thinking,
but in a completely new sense. It is as if one were to look at a
previously established universe from the angle of one's own, i.e.
from the individual's perspective. In this perspective rationality
is still the way to the understanding of the world, but this time it is
handled in a different way. Rationality becomes individualized
rationality, departing very often from the authoritatively established universe of discourse to lend expression to the experience of
the world as it presents itself to struggling smaller groups or to the
lonely individual. If I propose to call this rationality, by comparison with Thomist Rationality, an Individualized Rationality,
I am aware of the fact that the difference between them needs
further elaboration. But there seems to me no doubt that modern
experimentalism is born out of this individualized rationality
which does not accept a pre-established system of metaphysics,
but is ready to change the hypothesis if new facts and unexpected
experiences do not fit into the scheme. The most fruitful methodo-
logical device in science, namely to adjust if necessary our whole
system of thought to the ever-broadening sphere of experience,
becomes, when applied to human life and moral issues, the
greatest predicament of modern man. By developing the same
kind of dynamic rationality in the moral world, modern man
tends to lose a firm basis on which to stand. Whereas in some
prominent individuals this falling into the abyss of the self without
reaching the bottom presents itself as a grandiose struggle, a new
Titanism, in the average man the very same dynamics lead to a
frivolous attitude of believing in nothing and to an endless
craving for new sensations. At present I cannot do more than
point to these two types of rationality. It is very likely that the

future will have to be devoted to their reconciliation, and only one thing can be forecast: a simple evasion of the calamity of the modern mind will not do, but neither can bottomless individualism be made the basis of social organization.

(4) *The Meaning of Religious and Moral Recommendations in a Democratically Planned Order*

If we agree that religion will not, and cannot, be a department of a planned society, but must once again come alive both in the motivations of individual actions and embodied in institutions, we do not plead for a religious form of totalitarianism. Just the opposite is desired, and as long as we are democrats and plan for the sake of freedom, all our thinking must be deeply concerned with avoiding that danger. A totalitarian planning in which Goebbels and Himmler were to be replaced by a Christian clericalism would be equally disastrous. It would be detrimental to Christianity itself, it would kill its very soul, since complete externalization and formalism would ensue. Planning for Freedom, although conscious of the need for greater unity and a common purpose, can only open a chance to every source of deeper regeneration, but it cannot superimpose a creed, whatever it may be. It is better for the Christian faith itself if it is not identified with one party but carries its spirit into all. It is not quite easy at the present stage to foresee what that non-totalitarian penetration of the religious spirit into society will be, because that is not only a matter of analysis but a creative process which cannot be foreseen in its details. And those who think that planning can lay down the rules of social and spiritual change in advance forget once more that Planning for Freedom is planning the scope for experiment and growth. What can be attempted, however, in order to further the right sort of solution is to lay down first what a genuine religious penetration cannot and should not be like.

(*a*) It is obvious from what we have said before that a planned society cannot be built on the neutralized attitudes of the late Liberal age, in which all the values tended to cancel each other out.

(*b*) On the other hand, it is obvious that an imposition of values by a central authority cannot be satisfactory to a modern secular society, even if it were done by a religious authority. From that, two requirements follow: (i.) That the generally accepted values must be based upon tacit or explicit consensus. In the past, custom represented such a tacit consensus, and where this is vanishing and can no longer be maintained, it becomes necessary that new methods must be developed, in which persuasion, imitation, free discussion and consciously accepted example will play a rôle. (ii.) That it is not necessary to enforce basic consensus on more complicated issues in those spheres in which individual creed or free experimentation are the best promoters. Here we can learn from Liberalism that the highest forms of spiritual life flourish best in Freedom. To put it quite briefly, we must establish a set of basic virtues such as decency, mutual help, honesty and social justice, which can be brought home through education and social influence, whereas the higher forms of thought, art, literature, etc., remain as free as they were in the philosophy of Liberalism. It must be one of our main concerns to establish the list of those primary virtues without which no civilization can exist, and which make for that basic conformity which gives stability and soundness to social life. This does not mean that the Churches as such should not make recommendations about what they feel to be a Christian social order, or about what they think Christian art, philosophy or morality should be. But it makes all the difference whether insight is propagated in terms of recommendations or superimposed by force.

The more the age of planning proceeds, the more it will become likely that these recommendations will take the shape of a consistent system similar to the Summa of St. Thomas, for the simple reason that in a non-planned society there is less coherence between the various phases of behaviour than in a planned society. As far as liberal society is based upon free competition and continual individual adjustment, the variety of possible responses is considerable. There is only the possibility of giving general advice as to right and wrong. One can convey the principle but not the concrete pattern. In a dynamic and free society, there is a special premium on the capacity of coping with the unexpected, producing new responses and being able to take the initiative and responsibility in enterprises involving risk. The scope for all that diminishes in a planned society: one can not only reasonably foresee the simpler patterns of behaviour, but even those of consistent conduct. Religious and moral recommendations, as we have called them, will therefore tend not only to lay down some principles, but also a set of concrete patterns of behaviour, the image of satisfactory social institutions and a whole world view as a connecting link between them. Again, as long as they are not meant as dictatorial rules set down by a minority for the many, but as the fruits of creative imagination put at the disposal of those who crave for a consistent way of life, there is not only no harm in them, but they actually fulfil a function without which modern society cannot survive.

(5) *The Move towards an Ethics in which the Right Patterns of Behaviour are more positively stated than in the Previous Age*

This means at the same time that the predominance of the so-called formalistic ethics over the material ethics comes to an end. When speaking of formalism in ethics, we think of those ethical rules which deliberately refrain from giving concrete advice in terms of what ought to be done, but instead confine themselves to an abstract formulation of the idea of right and wrong action. The best example of this is the Kantian maxim which, instead of saying "Do this or that," sets down the general formal rule, "Act as though the principle of your action might become the principle of action in general." In my view, this type of ethics corresponds to a social order in which it is hardly possible to foresee the concrete patterns of right action. The philosopher lived in a phase of history in which society was completely in the re-making; in a society based upon expansion and constant dynamics, pioneering and exploration of new fields. This is the world of early Capitalism and Liberalism, in which free competition and individual adjustment defined the scope of relevant action, and where a concrete pre-determination of the patterns of right action would deprive man of that elasticity which is the main requirement of survival in a rapidly changing world.

Although Kant, who lends expression to the formalization of the new ethics, is himself unaware of the sociological foundations of his thought, it is legitimate to say that he arrived at that formalizing concept mainly because he lived in a society such as we have just described, in which the pre-determination of the relevant patterns of action would have meant limiting the freedom of the pioneering individual. As contrasted with his age the mediaeval system of ethics developed in a society with moderate dynamics and with institutions regulated mainly by tradition. In it a concrete "material" determination of the "right" patterns of action in advance was not unfeasible.

To the modern shift to formalism corresponds the tendency towards laying all the moral emphasis not upon objective and overt behaviour and its visible consequences, but upon the intention of the doer. It is again Kantianism which is the clearest expression of that *Gesinnungsethik* which, of course, is historically nothing more than an elaboration of the Protestant idea that conscience is the essential thing in action. Sociologically speaking, this exclusive emphasis on the motives of the person acting corresponds to a world in which there is little chance to predict even the most immediate consequences of any action, as one lives in a society entirely unplanned and, in addition to that, in one which is steadily expanding, changing and transcending frontiers, and is characterized by great social mobility and a fusion of cultures. It is interesting to note that what Max Weber [3] called *Verantwortungsethik* (as contrasted with the pure *Gesinnungsethik*), that is a morality which expects you to foresee at least some of the immediate consequences of your actions and be responsible for them, is of late increasingly coming to the fore. This seems to happen because in our society areas of free adjustment are diminishing: instead of them, through the organization of so many fields of action, spheres develop where standard patterns prevail, and it becomes possible to envisage at least the immediate consequences of one's activities. Consequently responsibility for them becomes a reasonable demand. To formulate once more the correlation: Formalism and *Gesinnungsethik* correspond to a stage in which the ethical and the active person is bound to remain society-blind, because there is less scope for pre-calculation than in a society which is nearing the stage of planning or which is already planned: where key positions exist, the pressing of a button implies foreknowledge of certain results. Of course, this does not mean that there is no scope for chance and fate, but there are fields in which, for a while at least, the process of adjustment through trial and error and conflict is replaced by pre-established patterns.

(6) *The Tension between the Private and Parochial World on the one hand and the Planned Social Order on the other*

In many ways, therefore, the ethical rules of behaviour and conduct will again become more concrete, and in that more like the Thomistic idea of a concrete system. On the other hand, if we do not emphasize the Protestant tradition sufficiently (that only through the inner experience and the voice of conscience can right behaviour be sanctioned), this objectivism may lead to the very dehumanization which characterizes the totalitarian dictatorships, where the final responsibility for right and wrong lies with the Führer or the Gauleiter, or with the planning commission. The danger of exacting too much subservience in the religious sphere is that the very same pattern of blind allegiance may prepare the ground for blind submission to non-religious forces. The Lutheran type of Protestantism undoubtedly contributed to a frame of mind which, more easily than the Calvinist, submits to dictation in worldly affairs.

It is very difficult to answer the question as to how we shall reconcile, in a planned society, where the pre-established patterns of conduct are bound to prevail, the necessary objectivism with a certain amount of subjectivism according to which the value of action consists in the share which individual conscience and choice have in it. The possible remedy of this dilemma may be sought: (*a*) In an education which again and again brings home to the acting individual the real meaning of the whole pattern of society, and remains dissatisfied as long as the individual only mechanically fulfils his partial tasks. In these cases, social awareness becomes a moral obligation. It is only now that we realize how detrimental it was that democracy, even where its institutions functioned smoothly, failed to rouse that deep interest in its achievements which alone makes living in a social order a genuine experience. Democracy in these countries became a matter of routine and habit, and it is only to be hoped that the challenge of totalitarianism will bring about that process of revitalization in which institutions which have formerly simply been taken for granted will once more become a matter of conscience.

(*b*) It may not always be possible to engage the whole personality in the action patterns of a social order, as there are too many things mechanically arranged for the individual; yet it is still possible, and even necessary, in a democratically planned society that the question of conscience should come alive whenever one decides on the acceptance of a new plan, or whenever one feels responsible for its being put into practice after the decision has been taken. In this sense it is very likely that the crucial tests for the individual conscience will not always, as in the past, be found in the little decisions of our everyday activities, but in our taking the responsibility for decisions concerning the social order at large. That means that in the past it was not quite impossible to say: "As long as I am a fairly good Christian in my private life, in my personal relationships, I need not worry too much about the social and political order in which I live." This attitude will become entirely impracticable in a society in the stage of planning, because there the organization of the framework of society to a large extent determines what is possible in private relationships. If society is planned not for freedom but on totalitarian lines, complete withdrawal into the parochial and personal world is virtually impossible. Thus the social organization becomes more than ever a matter of personal conscience. One cannot be a good Christian in a society where the basic rules are against the spirit of Christianity. If it was already true in Tolstoy's day, who said that serfdom was anti-Christian not only because it compelled the serf to remain sub-human but also because it compelled the landlord to behave as a non-Christian, it is even more true to-day when there are no private nooks and corners which remain unaffected by the prevailing principles of social organization.

Although it is obvious that we shall have to do everything to keep personal relationships alive, to support the spontaneous growth of small groups within the framework of planned society, all these remedies will not help unless a completely new emphasis is laid upon the control of social structure at large. It is more than ever a matter of conscience for the Churches to test the basic principles of social organization in the light of Christian values.

(7) *Ethical Rules must be tested in the Social Context in which they are expected to work*

If this be true, it is obvious that in taking a stand on current problems, especially on Planning, a much greater sociological awareness is needed than ever before. From now on, in order to be able to judge how a proposal will work and whether it is worthy to be called Christian, one needs to have a concrete vision of how society works.

It is therefore necessary for Christian thinkers more intimately to blend theological thought with sociological knowledge. The meaning of a norm becomes concrete only if one refers it to the context in which it works. Without that social frame of reference the norm remains empty. The contextualization of moral codes is, therefore, one of the outstanding tasks. To give a concrete example: Whether a rule is Christian or not can perhaps, under present conditions, best be judged by a social worker, teacher or a parish minister, for very often they alone are able to watch the working of a norm under modern conditions in, let us say, slum life or among the unemployed. In other cases an expert in politics or business might be called in to state what a regulation really means in his sphere of life. A rule may sound very Christian in the abstract; in the concrete it may produce opposite results. In these cases only those who have access to the concrete context of life are able to observe how social norms are reflected in the inner experience of the individuals concerned, and may be the judges of the real value of the norm. This is the reason why I am inclined to think that a redirection of habits and codes will have to be made in the future in consultation with sociologists and other experts. Their information will bring home to us how rules work in practice; the final recasting of norms will still be left to the theologian and the philosopher.

(8) *Can Sociology, the Most Secularized Approach to the Problems of Human Life, co-operate with Theological Thinking?*

This immediately raises another crucial issue equally concerning the nature of the co-operation between the theologian and the sociologist. How far is the theologian allowed to share the experimental attitude of the sociologist concerning values? If one takes the radical view that Christian values are eternal and pre-established, there is little chance for co-operation. Only if there is at least a limited scope left for experimentalism in the field of valuations is it possible to make use of the sociological approach. It is no good hiding the difficulties arising in this

sphere, and therefore, in order to make the challenge complete, I
shall represent the sociological approach in its most radical form.

Sociology in its historical origins is a secularized, perhaps the
most secularized, approach to the problems of human life. It
borrows its strength from following up to its final consequences
the immanent, i.e. the non-transcendental, approach to human
affairs. It does not only avoid relying on God as an explanation
for things as they are or ought to be, but does not refer, as long
as it uses its tools consistently, to absolute superhuman entities.
This becomes particularly apparent when it deals with values.
The idealist philosopher, even if an atheist, will still refer to some
values as eternal entities in a platonic sense. The sociologist
would be inconsistent if he were to start by accepting certain
values as being beyond the historical social process. What he
wants to find out is how far the variability of social phenomena,
including the prevailing valuations, are functions of the changing
social process. To him it would seem unwise and methodo-
logically inconsistent to exclude certain phenomena from the
range of sociological explanation. He would not agree to a
suggestion which considers certain phenomena from the very
outset as being holy and therefore not open to the sociological
approach, whereas others, being profane, could be more accessible
to it. This is the line many of those take who realize that one
could learn a great deal from sociology but who are afraid of
deprecating religious themes by exposing them to the profaning
effect of empirical analysis. The danger of this half-way solution
is, firstly, that it breaks the dynamic *élan* of the sociological
approach, which consists in the radical exploration of the social
forces operating in history, and secondly, that it cannot be satisfactory to be told in advance what can be grasped in terms of
empirical analysis and what cannot. In my view, it is more
sincere and profound to allow the sociologist to develop his concepts, hypotheses and methods as fully as possible and see how
far they go. It is wiser for the theologian to take from him
whatever seems to be evident in the light of his interpretation
and try to understand with him the whole range of human
behaviour and valuations as problems of individual and group
adjustment. And only then, when the method will have done
its best, will it automatically reveal its limitations. It will become
obvious how much of human behaviour and valuations can be

understood in terms of the categories of function and where it is necessary to go beyond these categories.

In this light the proposed method of co-operation between sociology and theology seems more sincere and efficient than the previously mentioned half-hearted one. Of course, this sort of co-operation became feasible only at the end of the epoch of Liberalism, when extreme Rationalism had run its course and the axiomatic limitations of the different types of rational analysis in human affairs became apparent to those who used them. By having carried through the sociological analysis to its final consequence [4] the sociologist himself sees where other approaches need to be called in to supplement his findings. On the other hand, before they have embodied the knowledge available through the sociological analysis, philosophy and theology seem to deal with a picture of life which is deprived of those problems and findings which are most characteristic of our age.

(9) *The Concepts of Christian Archetypes*

Looking at the problem from the angle of the theologian, the question will be how much scope experimentalism will be allowed within the framework of religious thinking. If one takes the attitude that the truth of Christianity is laid down in certain clear-cut statements which have supra-temporal validity, there will be small scope for sociological thinking. In this case, the sources of error only can be revealed with the help of sociological analysis. If this approach is chosen, sociology will only be useful as an instrument to make it intelligible why certain groups are incapable of understanding the truth one possesses. If in contrast to this one holds the view that the fundamental Christian attitudes have not been laid down in terms of rigid rules, but have rather been given in concrete paradigmata which only point in the direction where Right is to be sought, then there is scope left for creative contribution in every new epoch. History will then consist in materializing that Christian substance according to the changing social setting in which the generations of men are called to live. Characteristically the archetypes of Christian attitudes were not formulated in terms of abstract commands but are revealed in the parables which tell us about Christ's life and teaching. A parable never gives the distilled, abstract principles of an exemplary conduct, but speaks through a concrete image

E

containing the whole historical and social setting in which it occurred. But this evidently does not mean that the very same setting will last for ever; thus the Christian is compelled to transfer the intention of Christ into varying situations. As long as the changes in the historical situation are relatively simple, common sense might suffice to adapt the meaning of the archetype to the new situation. But the more society becomes complex, the more sociological knowledge is needed for the understanding of the real meaning of the changed historical context, and for the adequate reinterpretation of the normative image. The advantage of having inherited the norm in the idiom of concrete images and not in terms of abstract principles is that it helps us to avoid formalism. Every rational formulation of a principle is misleading, as it tempts us to logical deduction, where intellectual consistency remains the only criterion of truth; whilst a concrete image in one stroke conveys to us overt behaviour, inner motivations, the image of concrete personalities and the concrete social context in which all that occurred. In one word, it communicates the whole wealth of religious experience, which is always more than the purely rational and functional aspects of life.

As long as the wealth of religious experience is kept alive by continuous reference to the original images of Christian experience, another danger of sociological thought, that it might degenerate into a passion for dismembering whole configurations and genuine experiences into abstract devices, is also removed. There is all the difference between using the tools of analysis for the sake of clarification and greater awareness in the medium of an experience which precedes that analysis, and between an analysis which comes from nowhere and leads nowhere. Analysis for the sake of increased awareness is the thing needed to-day, for neither pure instinct nor unenlightened intuition can help us in a situation as involved as ours.

If this interpretation of Christian Truth be correct, namely, that it is only given as a direction and not as a rigid prescript, then two important sociological characteristics of a norm can be demonstrated on it. On the one hand, it leaves open great scope for adaptation, and on the other it prevents man from getting lost in the endless possibilities of changing his behaviour which ultimately are bound to lead to the disintegration of personality and society.

This sociological problem is most clearly reflected in the dilemma of any planned society. The latter can neither allow its basic issues to be exposed to boundless reinterpretation nor to become so dogmatic that through it the experimental attitude towards change disappears. There will, therefore, in every planned society be a body somehow similar to the priests, whose task it will be to watch that certain basic standards are established and maintained. On the other hand, provision must be made for social opportunities which foster the growth of absolutely free thought, whatever the risk may be that goes with it. We should never forget that the brief spells of free thought in history fell in those periods when clerical bodies had lost the exclusive monopoly of interpreting the meaning of life and human affairs. Freedom of thought and the marvellous development of the experimental spirit in Greece are due to the fact that nothing like an Oriental hierarchy could develop there. In the Renaissance and in the age of Liberalism the free competition between Churches and sects and free groups of intellectuals brought about that fermentation in the medium of which science and free personality developed.

The Anglo-Saxon pattern of Planning for Freedom can therefore fall back neither on the mediaeval pattern of clericalism nor upon the totalitarian State-imposed creeds. Planning here will primarily consist in providing the scope and opportunities for the growth of dissenting, sect-like social formations, and the growth of a free intelligentsia without allowing that the very same freedom should degenerate into anarchy. The translation of these demands into institutional guarantees will have to be one of the main topics of further thinking.

PART II. CHRISTIAN VALUES AND THE CHANGING ENVIRONMENT

(1) *The Methods of Historical Reinterpretation. The Passing and the Lasting Elements in the Idea of Progress*

In the period of changes lying before us the central problem of Christian thought will probably be: How does the application of Christian values change with the social and economic environment? This question in all its magnitude can only be solved in life itself. But this process of personal and collective experience will bear fruits only if it is constantly guided by conscious thinking. What we want is not only abstract thought, which relies exclusively on the method of logical deduction, but a kind of thinking which receives its main incentives from a concrete casuistry, from watching the predicament of Christians in an environment entirely different from that in which Christian experience was first formulated.

Thus, the task will be to discover whether and how far the same spirit can permeate situations entirely different from those in which it originally emerged. Such a permeation of the new situation takes place through the solution of the current conflicts of life. Conflicts are, rightly understood, symptoms of a discrepancy between established forms of attitudes and valuations and the changing situation. By solving these conflicts in a Christian spirit, both a partial spiritualization of the new environment and a reinterpretation of the very same spirit takes place. This process of living reinterpretation is continually going on; it was already present when early Christian groups had to give up their chiliastic hopes that the end of the world and the coming of the kingdom of God were imminent. This change of mind and a realistic acceptance of certain facts modified nearly everything in the attitudes and conduct of these groups, and yet they emanated from the very same spirit at a different stage. As long as groups are small and the situation relatively simple, the experience of such groups is able unconsciously to carry out the task of reinterpretation. Only when the complexity of civilization makes these reinterpretations very involved is it necessary that men of religious experience and experts of social change join in the work of reinterpretation. Even at this complex level the real reinterpretation is done through group life, and the men of religious experience and the experts have only a say if they are participants in that shared experience. Their findings will be based upon discussion, but it will have to be a discussion which, instead of blindly collecting or summarizing facts and valuations, explores, as it were, the nature of the predicament commonly experienced.

The possession of shared experience and the knowledge of casuistry will, however, only yield results if the questioning mind is aware of the deeper implications of the enquiry. First, one will have to be aware of the fact that in our age different ways of thinking prevail, and that they have different effects on the method of re-valuation itself. In this respect there are two extremes. One is the rather rigid attitude which identifies

Christianity with one particular epoch of its history, whereas the other somehow consciously or unconsciously applies the pattern of "Progress" to the sphere of valuations. The significance and the value of these methods has to be made conscious before one applies them. Without awareness of their nature and of their limitations there is a danger of being mastered by a method of thought instead of mastering it.

If we want to avoid the first error we must be aware of the historical variations of Christian attitudes in the past. By that same awareness one can avoid the other pitfall of taking as Christian only the more recent elaborations of Christian thought and life. It is, for example, important to recall which were the Christian virtues and attitudes which came to the fore during the development of Capitalism, and which elements in Puritanism corresponded to the requirements of the new era rather than to the essentials of Christian inheritance.[5] This might lead to re-valuations, e.g. to the re-valuation of asceticism or of certain aspects of it. In these cases, sociological awareness of the historical variations of the Christian theme would lead not to a kind of relativism but to a liberation of creative intuition, which develops adequate responses to a changing environment out of the same fundamental sources.

It is obvious that this attitude to history is different from that embodied in the liberal idea of progress or in its religious equivalent, Modernism. They share in a way the attitude that the really important things are those which happened in the last few hundred years, and that the longer time goes on the more progress there will be, and that therefore everything that is old must, like an old-fashioned dress, be renovated if it is to survive. This basic attitude, which has characterized the modern mind, is rapidly being altered by the perception of the evident deterioration of moral standards in a monopoly-capitalist and totalitarian world. It is clearly untrue that we are automatically progressing and that the Churches and the religious mind ought to hasten to adjust themselves to all the novelties of the age. This disillusionment with one's own age has already, it is true, gone so far that it substitutes for belief in the future the creed that everything is better because it is old, and that one ought to superimpose upon a modern world various attitudes and institutions belonging to the past. In its most dangerous form it leads to a kind of

"Pétainism" which seeks to overcome the evils of modern society by cloaking it in the pageantry of the past (*Le Régime des Notables*).

Now that the idea of progress has lost its glamour, it is all the more important to realize the elements of truth that it contains.   Firstly, science and technique, including the social techniques, follow an upward line.   They continually improve by further correction of mistakes, by enlarging the body of knowledge and understanding, by continually recasting the hypotheses which organize that increasing knowledge and by improving their efficiency.   The error of the philosophy of progress was that it transferred that pattern of historical development, i.e. the idea of rectilinear rise, to the evolution of the moral consciousness and of culture.   I think that Alfred Weber [6] was right when he said that culture radiates from a focus but does not develop in a straight line.   If this is true, Modernism was right in so far as it insisted that the religious thinker should be up to date in science and should not hamper its development, but it was wrong in trying directly to include religious life in the pattern of progress.

The other element of truth in the idea of progress which needs to be preserved is that for a living being "presentness" is of genuine value, and that this presentness is by no means self-contained, but exists as continual tension directed towards a state to come.   This dynamic element in presentness makes it impossible to interpret conservatism or traditionalism as a simple repetition of old situations or as the suppression of new conflicts with old formulae.   Presentness in the sphere of moral, religious and cultural experience means continual return to central experiences which transfuse their spirit into new situations.   Thus it means continual rebirth, a continual re-valuation and reinterpretation of the same substance.   This reinterpretation is, on the one hand, more than an intellectual task, because it appeals to genuine experiences, to our capacity for intuition and creative imagination.   On the other hand, rightly understood, it mobilizes the deepest resources of the intellect, because reorientation in such a complex world as ours can only be achieved with the help of philosophical, sociological and other knowledge.

(2) *Planning and Religious Experience*

While it is obvious that it is impossible to-day to be consistently religious without a great deal of awareness and intellectual knowledge, and without contact with political action, it is equally true that there are dangers in applying the scientific and technical attitude directly to human affairs. It is the predicament of our age that we realize that planning is necessary, but also know that wrong planning may be disastrous. It has always been open to question how far institutions can foster religious experience. In an age of planning, when the number of institutions is increasing, and these institutions are being co-ordinated, the problem becomes still more acute. On the other hand, even those who look at planning with the eyes of the engineer, and are inclined to believe that their approach to social affairs is all-embracing, realize that the purely technical and functional view is incomplete, and that when society is directed by purely utilitarian motives it lacks an inner dynamic. In times of prosperity and peace it looked as if man could live on Hollywood and ice-cream soda alone, but now that mankind is engaged in a life-and-death struggle for civilization even the engineer realizes that society is rooted in deeper layers of the human soul than he ever thought. It is particularly important that this country should become aware of this problem, since it is her destiny to lead the revolt of all the suppressed peoples.

The meaning of our question, therefore, is what can be done to restore these forces of deeper origin before the whole community is destroyed? How can we plan it so as to encourage the free flow of these forces and to allow their spiritual power to permeate the whole of life?

The following attitudes to planning are possible in regard to the relevance of planning to these deeper religious experiences:

(*a*) One of absolute hostility—that any institutionalization and planning is detrimental.

(*b*) The equally radical attitude that only through direct attack on the problem, strict regimentation, orthodox control, detailed casuistry, will they survive.

(*c*) That the conditions under which these deeper experiences will flourish can be planned.

(3) *The Meaning of Planning for Freedom in the case of Religious Experience*

I think that the first two attitudes are not very helpful to us whose ideal is Planning for Freedom, that is, to plan society for the sake of the spontaneity of life. Therefore it seems all the more important to investigate the different meanings of the third approach in the case of religion.

Planning for those deeper religious experiences may simply mean that, while we plan for everything else, free scope is left for religion so that it can arise spontaneously. This is not laissez-faire, because it means keeping a careful watch on the conditions which may obstruct religious experience and practice.

The next attitude is that it is untrue that by creating a vacuum religious experience is automatically drawn from the soul. The force which awakens it is tradition. If you destroy the social framework of tradition you destroy the conditions of religious experience. For those who hold this view it will be an extremely important task to enumerate some of the main elements of tradition. Is it reverence for what is old or is it habit, is it imitation or is it spiritual contagion, or is it an as yet unexplored transfer of unconscious formative energies which lend a specific shape and meaning to the various phases of human experience?

Others may say tradition is not enough. Tradition does not exist *in vacuo*, it is linked up with certain social conditions. These have to be maintained in order to maintain the corresponding tradition. Those who desire to maintain the peasantry because they have a certain type of religious tradition, or those who oppose the destruction of the solitude of the small workshop or are against the aggregation of masses because it gives rise to crowd behaviour, argue in this way.

Yet others may hold that the survival of religious experience is not dependent on immediate surroundings and social groups but on the whole pattern of society, because that is what fosters or suppresses deeper experiences. It is the family, the church, the school, business life and public opinion, the factory and the workshop, art and literature and their mutual relations, which foster or hamper the deeper experiences in man.

Again, others may say that what really matters is personal inspiration, and that the task is therefore to create the conditions for it. We must create a society in which personal relationships carry weight, in which there is scope for free fellowship in which personality as a whole is engaged, and where the person with a real vocation has a chance and natural leadership comes into its own. The sociological problem is as follows: Is this possible under the artificial conditions of big cities where people live in inarticulate masses, where neighbourhood has lost significance, where they cannot follow up the fate of their fellow-men, where, therefore, the life-history of the individual loses its paradigmatic meaning? The deepest kind of religious truth was perhaps, under more natural conditions, conveyed through the example of the life of a saint or a sage or a wise ruler, just as the life-stories of Christ or of Job are more unforgettable than narrow precepts, maxims or theological abstractions. This applies also to situations which lose their symbolic value in the crowded existence of a big city, where we meet as a rule for highly abstract businesslike purposes or for forms of enjoyment which seldom convey deeper common experience. Under more primitive conditions significant situations like birth, marriage and death reminded men of the transcendental forces of life. In our society they lose that meaning as soon as they become nothing but a tiresome item in our time-table.

(4) *The Four Essential Spheres of Religious Experience*

The answer to all these questions of where institutional interference and deliberate planning can do something for the growth of religious life will, of course, largely depend on a previous decision, that is to say on what we regard as the essence of religious experience. If I had to summarize the most important views about the essence of religion I should mention the following:

(*a*) One may hold that the substance of religion is to be found in personal communion with God. Then one will be inclined to think with certain mystics that nothing else in life really matters and that you cannot plan for it. Nevertheless, even mystics have known that there are certain conditions favourable or adverse to this experience. The invention of monastic life is only another expression of the truth that the religious contact with the superhuman is strictly linked up with certain external conditions. The recognition of the fact that monastic religious life is compatible with some types of work but not with others, reveals great sociological and psychological wisdom. Monks were allowed to plough or to live as beggars, but commercial activities seemed to create a mental state which tended to distract the mind from its religious vocation. Thus one can plan, if planning is rightly interpreted, even for ecstatic

E*

experience. It will become more and more a question whether something corresponding to the monastic seclusion, some form of complete or temporary withdrawal from the affairs of the world, will not be one of the great remedies for the dehumanizing effects of a civilization of busybodies. If this is so, this monastic seclusion will once more have two functions. The first will be to provide an opportunity for those who, so to speak, specialize in religious experience, and whose one task is to transmit the spirit once revealed to later generations without themselves making the adjustments to the new surroundings. These will be the guardians of the spirit, to whom the purity of the deeper experience is more important than its contemporaneity. But there will be, secondly, more secular "orders" into which the active politician and business man can withdraw for a while for contemplation, and so make contact with those who are less involved in the struggle for existence. The man of the world will then have the task of translating that inspiration into the language of contemporary thought and practice. Modern society needs the counter-weight of solitude to the crowd experience. It is one of the features of the Russian Communist experiment that it is hostile to anything like privacy. England more than any other country has the opportunity, when entering the age of planning, to transfer the desire for privacy and solitude to the pattern of a planned society. But it is imperative that one should not confuse mere despiritualized seclusion, e.g. sitting by the fireside in dullness and boredom, with the solitude which is a necessary condition for higher religious experience. The debased form of solitude may hide even worse forms of emptiness than the noises of the crowd.

(b) Others will feel that the real religious experience is present only in personal relationships, that where two or three are gathered together in the name of God, God is present. Mutual help, personal inspiration are more important for such people than the refined and artificial practices of the mystic, who in his supreme egotism withdraws from the world. Those who share this opinion will, of course, focus their planning activities on the restoration of neighbourhood and fellowship.

(c) Others may hold that one of the essentials of religious reality is incorporated in the pattern of social life. The subjective aspect of religious experience may be very important, but it is short-sighted not to see that part of its reality exists in the social edifice, which may conform to a right or wrong pattern and may either be full of the spirit or bare of it. The social pattern is more than the sum of the activities of atomized units; man consciously or unconsciously works on that pattern. The citizens of the Greek cities sensed it, the great empire-builders, the ancient Romans and the English, put the best of their powers into that achievement. If the pattern is permeated by the spirit, there is a continuous give-and-take between the individuals and the pattern. The individual invests his best powers in it, but receives forces greater than his own, because it is the integrated inspiration of the whole community which responds. It is like the collective building of a cathedral, which is a collective work of art, where the contribution of even the greatest genius remains anonymous, since he can never tell where his contribution begins or how much of what he considers as his own is inherited or due to a more than individual impulse.

If an individual partakes in that kind of society his achievements will generally reach a higher level than if he were to live on his own spiritual resources alone. The advantage of living in such a social pattern which embodies the spirit is that the individual can never fall below a certain level. (The tragedy of Germany is that it did not succeed in establishing a real society in that sense.) The danger of living in a society with an established pattern is that the individual, living beyond his individual resources, may give up struggling because, following the ritual and having the proper habits, he may lead an impeccable life without adequate exertion. The danger of a social pattern which embodies religious experience is that everything may gradually and imperceptibly become mere convention without anyone being able to say exactly when the deterioration begins. Those who think that it is the whole social pattern which really carries the individual will believe in some kind of collective salvation, and will pay at least as much attention to the improvement of the social structure as to the improvement of the conditions for individual salvation through personal experience or through the creation of opportunities for fellowship.

It is important to notice that the Bolshevist ideal of society is in many ways a secularized form of this idea—redemption through the right social order.

(d) Again, there may be some who will feel that the real

guarantee of the continuation of religious life is to be sought in the persistence of the much-despised conventions. Regular church-going and services, the observance of a certain ritual, orthodoxy on basic issues, are taken as a better guarantee of survival than those doubtful inner experiences of which you can never know where they will lead. This is a kind of religious behaviourism which existed long before behaviourism as a psychological doctrine. Just as the latter thinks that the creation of suitable habits is more important for the survival of the social order than high-brow ideas and doctrines, so this kind of ritualistic orthodoxy sees the guarantee of religion in the religious forms of habit-making. There is a further analogy between psychological behaviourism and ritualistic orthodoxy, namely, the belief that man's experience works from the outside. The performance of religious duty creates a mould into which real energy may flow. However sound impulses may be, without a social and a religious mould they will evaporate. Those who hold this view will interpret planning for the religious life as concern for the formation of religious habits, and for organized opportunities for religious instruction and performance.

It is obvious from this analysis that planning for religion will mean different things according to the opinions held about the essence of religion. Each will look for a different remedy according to his particular religious philosophy. My personal conviction, which always inclines to a belief not in a patent remedy but in a variety of means, leads me to think that religion exists in all these forms and that a pluralist approach to planning will alone be satisfactory. In my view, a transmutation of the religious substance is continually at work. Religion in some phases exists on the level of purely personal experience, as it is conveyed by the mystics. Sometimes it flows into the mould of fellowship, sometimes it permeates the whole pattern of social organization, sometimes it hibernates in habits of thought and in petrified ritual practices. If this be true, the problem of planning for these things consists in realizing the variety of these forms as they coexist, and as they aid or hamper each other in their existence. You cannot plan for religion in the abstract, but you can plan for various concrete forms of religious life as described above. There are different remedies according to whether you feel that opportunities for privacy, inwardness and ecstasy have to be created or whether you feel that the right conventions are essential. Just as it is a general principle of right planning that there is no patent technique for planning, so is there none for planning the religious life. Just as in general there are certain spheres where the necessary activities have to be strictly organized and regimented, such as the organization of transport or the most efficient ways of rationing, so are there other spheres where room for organic growth has to be created and the weed of institutional deterioration has to be uprooted. It may very often be enough so to reorganize a community that a natural opportunity for fellowship, self-government, and spontaneity are preserved and the rest will then come by itself. Again, there are cases where everything depends on inspiration, and planning does not consist in institutional measures alone but in individual decisions. If there is a man with prophetic vision, he should be given his proper opportunity, or if there is a small sect or group which has an exceptional experience and the members of which find each other mutually stimulating, it should have the chance of exerting its influence in the right quarters. In this sphere the removal of special forms of frustration, the fight against the *vis inertiae* of vested interests, is more important than general regulations. Planning for Freedom is not a general regimentation but an elastic mould for the growth of society and consists in a differential use of the approaches. As applied to our problem of planning for religion, it means that planning will be different when the provision for the more rigid realities, as for instance habit-making or ritual, is our concern from what it will be when we deal with the substance of fellowship or personal inspiration, which cannot be directly controlled.

There is one more thing to bear in mind: although the different forms of religious substance coexist very often in society at large and have their proper share in the spiritualization of life, together they form a dynamic entity and in one historical period everything may depend on the intensity of personal experience and in another on the vitality of fellowship or tradition.

The survival of Great Britain depends on whether she is able to become not only a clearing-house of ideas and incentives but also a creator of a new vision, socially and spiritually, a vision of a better future which will give a lead to the peoples rising against universal aggression. At the moment there is still a general feeling of paralysis. In spite of Britain's stirring experiences her situation and that of the people who have faced the worst horrors of human existence are still widely apart in many respects. Britain is still in the midst of the painful process of revising habits of thought and emotional settings which grew and could prevail in an atmosphere of security and external stability.

If it comes, will the revival surge from the institutional sectors of religion? What do tradition and institutions really mean to people in whom Christianity is alive? Or is it more likely that all the emphasis will be on personal experience and fellowship? Is there a chance of a rebirth of popular religion within the churches, or will they in their rigidity expel from their ranks those who are able to cope with the new realities of the inner and outer world? In the latter case, there will again be heretics and sects who will live up to the requirements of the new age. On the other hand, a split of this kind in the face of a powerful and united enemy would be a dangerous venture, and everything which can make for a rebirth within the churches has to be seriously considered.

(5) *The Problem of Genuinely Archaic and of Pseudo-Religious Experience*

If one analyses the conditions of a rebirth of religious experience one has to mention the most radical view on the subject. It is not inconsistent to think that the rebirth of the religious substance may have to come from peoples untouched by our intellectual development, since the substance of religious experience is something genuine, and in this sense more primitive than is compatible with the analytical achievements of the modern mind. Intellectual history can be interpreted as the growth of a type of sophistication which gradually disintegrates the basic vision—those primeval images which are somehow the essential element of religious experience. An illustration of this theory of primitivism is found in the fact that although the philosophers and the intellectuals of late antiquity, e.g. the Stoics, were ready to accept a new spirit which transcended the life-patterns of antiquity, the new religious experience of Christianity was not the product of those sophisticated minds but emanated from the lower classes in Judea and from Oriental mystical sources. The theory of primitivism in the creative sense of the word is perhaps true, in so far as it makes us aware of the possible contribution of the Russians and other not fully Westernized groups to the rebirth of religious experience. It is not wholly impossible that what is happening in Russia, apart from conscious intention, is that a very genuine source of religious and primitive experience is using modern sophisticated terminology to translate itself into the idioms of modern society. Dostoiewsky translated archaic religious experiences, old traditions of Russian monastic life (cf. the character of the Starez Sossima) into the language of modern psychology. He realized ancient conflicts of the religious mind in modern situations. Thus his art is a marriage of genuine archaic, religious substance and modern forms of interpretation. Something like that is bound to happen if we want neither to relapse into sheer barbarism nor to "progress" into a despiritualized realm of mere analysis and sophistication.

With this in mind it is even more difficult to answer the question of what can be done to foster a rebirth out of the real depth of the soul. I think the way is, on the one hand, to be aware of the existence of the archaic potentialities in the mind and society and not to disregard them when they are at work, and on the other hand, clearly to distinguish those forms of intellectual activity which are instrumental, analytical and useful in the struggle for life from those which are intuitive, integrating and directly related to the deepest sources of human experience. No doubt these sentences lend themselves to misinterpretation. Every romantic attempt to discredit the positive aspects of modern thought, such as its rationalism, opposition to superstition and the critical spirit prevailing in it, may misuse this apologia of the non-rational powers to support a new mediaevalism, which is very often only a modern way of diluting an ancient substance. There is also the danger of worshipping the idols of barbarism under the cloak of a new primitivism. None the less, the possible misuse of a truth cannot prevent us from stating it. The only thing to do is to strengthen the sense of what is genuine in human utterances and to teach the new generation to discriminate between artificial surrogates and the real sources of spiritual regeneration.

(6) *Valuation and Paradigmatic Experience* [7]

We must now consider the relation between changing human valuations and the history of that genuine religious experience to which all observations of the previous paragraphs refer. Are

we discussing the nature of Christian valuations when we discuss
the transmutations of the religious substance and the institutional
means by which it can be kept alive?   What is the relation
between valuations and the basic experiences in which Christianity expresses itself?   We touch upon an old problem in a new
setting, we are thrown back upon the old controversies about the
relation between religion and morality.   We remember the
paradox that a man may be impeccable from the point of view
of morality and yet not religious, but we know also that an
immoral man can sometimes have deep religious experiences.
We also know that Christianity itself acknowledged the existence
of a moral code in the *ius naturale* (natural law), as being valid
although not permeated by the spirit.

From all this at least so much emerges, that Christian valuations will have two facets—the one which corresponds to the
fact that as values they have to regulate behaviour and conduct, and the other which corresponds to the fact that they
are the direct expression of a basic experience which need not
be shared by everybody.   To put it in another way: given
values can always be interpreted both as a means of adjustment to real situations, and as types of adjustment which are
directed by a particular *Weltanschauung*, i.e. by a few basic experiences which guide that adjustment.   If this be true, valuations
which do not solve the conflicts presented by the situations, i.e.
which do not solve problems of adjustment and thereby enable
us to act and live in a given world, are of no use.   On the other
hand, successful adjustment does not make the values by which
it has been guided into Christian ones or into the expression of
any other *Weltanschauung*.

The adjustment character of valuations makes it imperative
that they should change to a certain extent with the social
environment.   This aspect of valuations became gradually
understood by the Utilitarian Pragmatist philosophers, and one
can hardly deny the significance of that insight.   They saw that
neither the religious thinker nor the idealist philosopher is in a
position to realize that the business of living is a continuous
process of adjustment to ever-changing situations and that the
process of valuations is part and parcel of that process.   The
religious thinker and the philosopher focussed their attention
too much on one problem only, namely, on the justification of

the claim of a norm to be valid; they therefore raised only the question: "Why should commands be obeyed?" They did not ask how they could be obeyed if conditions from which they originally emerged have changed. This was exactly what interested the pragmatist, whose main question was: How does an advice or command solve the problems emerging from a new situation, and how does it produce, by adjustment, a new equilibrium out of the disequilibrium between an obsolete response and a changed condition, and how far do commands which are authoritative and preconceived solve emerging new difficulties? In their extreme experimentalism these philosophers very often rejected any pre-established regulative idea of conduct, because it prejudices spontaneous intelligent adjustment and cannot be modified in the light of consequences.

He who does not see the real significance of the challenge contained in these statements will never solve our problems and will hardly understand the real predicament of our age. On the other hand, those who think, as the pragmatists do, that they have already found an answer to the questions they raised, will equally remain blind to the real magnitude of the problem of valuations.

The difficulty in the pragmatist's answer is that it either identifies successful adjustment with right and wrong behaviour, or does not realize that by supporting individual spontaneity as the *absolute* claim he himself introduces unconsciously preconceived ideals of right conduct. In other words, the justification of a type of behaviour as being an efficient piece of adjustment to a given situation does not yet determine its being right or wrong from a Christian or a non-Christian point of view. The person who denies the significance of spiritual norms may adjust himself to certain demands of the social situation as well as the Christian does. What then is the difference between them? It can be found in the fact that the Christian does not simply want to adjust himself to the world in general or to the particle of environment in which he finds himself, but he wants to do so only in terms of an adjustment which, among other possible adjustments, is in harmony with his basic experience of life.

In this context it may be noticed that the philosophy and sociology of adjustment were first started as though there were only one efficient adjustment in a given situation. But the longer the variety of adjustments was observed, the more obvious it

became that, even on the plane of biological existence, adjustments to the same situation are bound to be different according to
the biological equipment of the respective animal or human
being. If there is a noise, the hare may run away and the frog
will stay put and hide. But a similar difference may be found
even among different individuals of the same species, and accords
with the psychological type to which they belong or with the
psychological tendencies which are dominant in them as the
result of their previous life-history. One child will make its
adjustment to an outward threat by hitting out, whereas another
child will withdraw.

Once the variety of adjustment types to the same situation
is admitted, only one more step is needed to realize that the
quality of adjustments may also be influenced by the *Weltanschauung* of the individuals or groups who make the adjustment
to the same situation. Hence, among the many efficient adjustments some may be Christian and some others not Christian.
It is clear that the adjustment quality of behaviour and conduct
guided by values must be present, if we understand by adjustment
not compromise (which is an unintelligent interpretation of the
word adjustment), but a response which in some way (if necessary
by fight and rebellion) settles the tasks presented by the situation.[8]
But the adjustment character of action does not describe it fully.
To it the *Weltanschauung* is to be added which is selective with reference to the existing types of adjustment patterns. It admits some
and rejects others. But what is the criterion of its selection? What
are the origins of its acceptance or refusal of certain ways of living,
acting and co-operation? Obviously, some basic experiences
which to the given *Weltanschauung* reveal the meaning of life in
general. In a *Weltanschauung*, just as in a religion, there are some
basic experiences which carry more weight than others, and which
are unforgettable in comparison with others that are merely passing sensations. Here is the answer to the question of the relation
between values and Christianity, between morality and religion.
The religious focus is not a moral or ethical experience, nor a
way of regulating behaviour and conduct, but a way of interpreting life from the centre of some paradigmatic experience. One
may discuss whether the basic Christian experience is original
sin, redemption, the liberating and creative power of love or
the Cross, the deeper meaning of suffering. It is from these foci

of experience that the adjustment patterns of right behaviour and conduct are always reinterpreted. If these paradigmatic experiences evaporate, as in secularized European history, it is obvious that the problem of values contains nothing but the adjustment character of human conduct. Right or wrong only means efficiency, and there is no answer to the question: Efficiency for what? Regulations and values are considered solely as means, and their ends are lost sight of. The only relevant criterion of right and wrong that remains can be deduced from the need for reconciling individual and group adjustment.[9] Only those adjustments of individuals are efficient which are compatible with the efficient adjustments of the groups to which they belong. On the other hand, those to whom the paradigmatic experiences are still relevant and alive but who do not realize the adjustment facet of values, are paralysed by the fact that they wish to apply the old devices literally to the new situations and fail to realize that without a translation of the genuine experiences into the idiom of the new situation they are doomed to failure. The problem of Christian values in a new environment consists in an awareness of the two aspects— an awareness of the paradigmatic basic experiences, and an intellectual awareness of the relevant changes in the modern environment.

(7) *The Sociological Meaning of Paradigmatic Experience*

Once the significance of paradigmatic experience has become apparent, it seems to provide a key to the understanding of what we usually mean by the "despiritualization" of modern life. It mainly consists in the evaporation of primordial images or archetypes which have directed the life-experience of mankind through the ages. Their appeal to the unconscious has been realized by historians of art and culture, by psychologists and philosophers.[10] Now that we see what happens when the power of these images wanes, we must add to the insight of those students the knowledge we can gain about their social significance.

To name a few of these archetypes or primordial images I may mention: the Hero, the Sage, the Virgo, the Saint, the Repentant; or, dominating the realm of Christian imagination: Baptism, Absolution, Agape, the Eucharist, the Good Shepherd, the Cross, Redemption. They are not fully understood if they

are taken as mere relics of a pre-scientific stage of development. It is their disappearance without anything else to take
their place which leads to the disintegration of modern life-
experience and human conduct. Without paradigmatic experiences no consistent conduct, no character formation and no
real human coexistence and co-operation are possible. Without
them our universe of discourse loses its articulation, conduct falls
to pieces, and only disconnected bits of successful behaviour
patterns and fragments of adjustment to an ever-changing
environment remain.

If the thought-model of adjustment to environment, which
produced so many important results in the field of biological
studies, is not only used as a hypothesis in the field of social
studies but is made a measuring-rod for human action, a dehumanization of life is bound to ensue. The scientific approach
produces its results by a complete elimination of those valuations
which are attached to things and the various forms of conduct
in social life. To those who act in life and are members of a
culture, values inhere in things. Those who act have continually
an ontological hierarchy in mind when they say, "This is bad,
this is good, this is better." The scientific approach rightly
starts with a neutralization of that ontological hierarchy in the
world of experience. To the psychologist one experience is as
important as any other; to the sociologist the social conditions
which produce a gangster are as relevant as the social conditions
which make for the development of a good citizen. As a method
of scientific research this neutral approach produces most valuable results, but if we try to make it a rule of conduct it becomes
a disintegrating force both in personal life and in the life of
society. It is scientifically justified to analyse both the experiences of a saint and of a hysteric as examples of psychological mechanisms; but deliberately to disregard the qualitative
differences in these experiences becomes detrimental for society
if it treats a saint as a hysteric or the hysteric as a saint. If there
are no paradigmatic experiences which induce us to lay different
emphasis on the different phases of action, there is no climax
towards which action will tend. This not only atomizes the life
of the individual and replaces the idea of a character by a
kaleidoscopic concept of life; it makes co-ordination of social
action equally impossible. Not only have paradigmatic ex-

periences and primordial images their function in the life of the individual as organizing principles of character formation, they are at the same time signposts in the co-operative activities of individuals.

Another facet of paradigmatic experiences is that they lend life a dramatic significance. Co-operation and common action in society are only possible where the same things mean more or less the same experience to everyone in society. He who does not share their meanings does not share the life of the community. But paradigmatic meaning is attached not only to static things but also to processes. Collective action will move towards a climax, and it is this dramatization which makes for real participation. Division of labour and division of functions without dramatization in a final common aim is like taylorization of work in the factory. It takes the meaning out of work which gives sense to the isolated or partial act. This is precisely what happens in our modern industrialized society. This pattern of taylorization, the meaningless dismemberment of co-operative tasks everywhere, destroys the primordial patterns of dramatized interpretation of life. It ultimately reduces the life-pattern of an individual to a well-arranged time-table, but any meaningful climax, any real direction, becomes "blacked-out" in the process.

The boundless accumulation of money, the endless striving for self-aggrandizement, the gigantic growth of the power complex, meaningless and conspicuous waste, which through the middle classes spread even to the lower classes, are but different aspects of the same process. A complete despiritualization of emotions which run amuck without any concrete purpose brings about a craving for but one satisfaction: to abreact. This is most conspicuous in the leisure attitudes of the many. "Let's go to the pictures or to a show, never mind what it is," so vague is the urge of men when their working day has come to its end. But this is only the inscription on the obverse of the medal—on the reverse we find the aimlessness of taylorized work.

We do not maintain that the masses of the past were more cultured: the opposite is true, they were more brutal and crude. But they did not suffer from the modern type of emptiness, nor has any previous culture tried to make their life-pattern the predominant one. It is obvious that the meaning of all this is not to put the blame on the masses. It is not their fault that their life was drudgery in the past, and that since the industrial revolution most of the pre-conditions of human living have gradually been destroyed. The Capitalist commercialization of leisure with its fostering of, and endless craving for, new sensations is as much responsible for the new type of mind as the wrong type of division of labour and social functions which creates partial tasks almost void of meaning. The question is not who ought to be blamed for all this, but what ought to be done about it, and how could something be done that does not remove symptoms on the surface only, but deals with the roots of the evil.

The presence of primordial images organizing conduct and collective action seems to be responsible for the fact that more primitive groups, like the Serbs, for instance, fight to the last ditch, whereas over-intellectualized nations give up fighting too easily. The genuine articulation of life-experiences which once emanated from religion and lent meaning to each item of our life has evaporated and nothing has taken its place, and to an atomized mind and an atomized society there remains nothing worth fighting for.

Considering this, it would be important to find out whether the Russians' determination to fight Hitler to the bitter end is still supported by the old religious paradigmatic experiences, or whether Bolshevism has succeeded in creating new images and a new dramatization of the common fate. If the latter is the case, it would not only prove anew how deeply the vision of the Brotherhood of Man is rooted in all human existence and how this vision can still draw fresh powers from very ancient sources, but also that even in our age, under certain conditions, new archetypes may be born.

For the very same reason it is far from me to say that the Humanitarian tradition from the Renaissance through the Age of Reason up to nineteenth-century Liberalism was void of paradigmatic experiences or lacking in vitality. The revolution against established authority, the indomitable courage to stand on one's own feet, the Titanism of accepting the burden of consciousness or of giving up hopes for a world beyond, were all tremendous dynamic powers in that development. But from the very outset their character was such as to remain powerful only as long as they expressed the drives present in ascending classes, and even in them they expressed mostly the mind of the pioneering few. The primordial images of the Humanitarian Renaissance and Liberal phase in history were in most cases symbols of dissension and individualization, and as such they were full of tension.

The corresponding frame of mind was far from irrationalism; it showed a deep inclination towards Reason. But the Ratio to which it had been devoted was fanatic. It only became tolerant, neutral and analytic after the classes, from which it emanated, had settled down and gained an established status in society.

The direction which was present in the fanatical, dynamic Ratio, and the images which were connected with it, evaporated. A sceptical, searching, analytical mind was left behind, apt to produce unbiassed fact-finding, but no longer able to define unifying purposes.

At the present juncture it is difficult to foresee what the trend of events will be, which of the two great *Leitmotifs* in our intellectual history will emerge as the predominant one. However, it is not quite impossible that the two forces will come to march in the same direction: those whose heritage was the religious spirit, to add depth and transcendence to human experience, and those who carried over from a great past the powers of Reason and the will to create a better world out of the potentialities of worldly resources. Perhaps the time is not too far distant when both will understand the meaning of the new great challenge of our time. Perhaps they will realize before long that they both have a new and extremely dangerous antagonist who dwarfs their internal differences. We know the name of this antagonist whose glaring shadow looms large all over our world. It is Mechanized Barbarism.

Even if they should fight a joint struggle and make common cause, it is not likely that the two forces will, and not even desirable that they should, totally merge. But it is possible that in spite of the tension which exists between them, or rather because of this tension, they might supplement each other and become aware that they really are two poles in the same battle of history destined to defend a common heritage.

(8) *Summing up. New Problems*

So far we saw, first, that a real understanding of the problems of Christian values in the changing environment calls for a clearer separation of the basic Christian experience from those developments of Christian belief and conduct which were the products of the Capitalist age.

Then we searched for a new interpretation of the philosophy of Progress in order to distinguish those elements in it which are still relevant, from others which appeared as linked up with expectations particular to a passing age. It is only salutary, we saw, if the optimism which thought of advance in all spheres of human affairs as a certainty should now be replaced by a more realistic outlook, which does not believe that mechanization and industrialization will automatically or by the miracle of dialectics produce better men or a happier society.

In the next stage of the argument it seemed desirable to clarify the meaning of such statements as "Planning for Religion." What is the possible meaning of such a claim? The answer to this question, so we argued, is relevant even beyond the religious sphere proper, as it may throw light on the more comprehensive enquiry into the meaning of planning in the spiritual sphere. The first reaction of all of us to the question whether one should plan for spiritual life is an energetic "No." But this is mainly due to an incapacity of understanding "Planning" as something different from the regimentation of the totalitarians. The discussion at once changes its character if, after some reflection, we have to admit that even in our present unplanned society we continually do something for education, art, science, religion, etc. There is, and there was, really no such thing as "non-interference" in these spheres. The novelty of the age of Planning, as we conceive it, will only be that the principles of the support given to the development and dissemination of culture will become clearer to us; should we aim at Planning for Freedom, we shall become even more scrupulous in the choice of the means through which the growth of spiritual life could be adequately fostered. This will lead to a much greater clarity concerning the nature of the substance and the possible transmutations of the substance for which we plan.

From the point of view of planning, an elaboration of two facets of Christian valuations seemed to be necessary. The first facet can be called the adjustment side in Christian valuations. Just as any other valuations, Christian valuations try to regulate attitudes, behaviour and conduct. And as such they have something to do with the adjustment character of human action to the environment, especially adjustment to a changing environment. Mostly, Christians are loath to admit the adjustment character of Christian codes of conduct. As I pointed out, this reluctance results either from a misinterpretation of the term "adjustment" (which does not mean "compromise," this being only one form of adjustment), or from the fact that Christian ethics very often emphasize the dignity of non-resistance. This again does not necessarily mean the negation of adjustment, but only a high appreciation of the non-aggressive forms of dealing with the problems of life. That Christianity in practice could not mean the opposite of adjustment, a disregard of concrete situations, can be proved by the fact that Christianity has survived. This actually meant that Christian men have made their adjustment to the ever-changing situation and that these adjustments were efficient, but they made them in most cases rather unconsciously. As long as the chiliastic expectations of the approaching end of the world prevailed, such a disregard for concrete situations may have been justified. But as soon as these hopes had to be postponed, and when finally the idea of History developed, the problem of living in a constantly changing world was ever present.

In my view, it is the strong point of Pragmatism as a philosophy that it makes the adjustment character of human behaviour quite explicit. This explicitness and honesty about what really happens in human action is not something for which this modern trend of thoughts ought to be blamed. It is from the moral point of view a higher form of living, which makes its adjustments to the changing conditions at the level of conscious rather than unconscious adaptation. As long as our adjustment is a conscious one, we are always in a position to state quite clearly and honestly: "As far as this I can accept the facts of a changed environment; here I have to stop and resist them." Adjustment to an undesirable situation will consist in a kind of action, individual and collective, which seeks remedy either by revolt or reform or else through emphatic temporary withdrawal from the arena of public action. A conscious admittance of the adjustment character of action makes it possible for the Christian to be progressive, to deal with the challenge of *res novae*, yet without becoming the victim of change. As the Christian has another source of direction for his activities beyond the mere desire of

adjustment and efficiency, he is always enabled to draw a de-
marcation line which indicates quite clearly which of the possible
types of adjustment are acceptable for him and which he must
reject.

It is here that the other facet of Christian valuation becomes
relevant, one which is beyond the reach of the pragmatist. This
other facet of Christian valuation (as a matter of fact, of any
valuation guided by a deeper purpose than mere survival and
some equilibrium with the surrounding world) is expressed in the
fact that the Christian does not merely want to adjust himself
to an environment, but wants to do so only through patterns of
action which are in harmony with his basic experience of life.
It is from this source that the traditionalist and conservative
element in Christian action emanates. Christian action has its
direction, since it is possessed with a basic vision of life, and
although this had continually to be reinterpreted it does not
wither away. This substance again and again focusses thought
and activity on certain issues and differentiates the otherwise
homogeneous challenges of the environment and the responses
to them into desirable and undesirable ones.

The significance of such a basic vision of life led us on to a
more thorough investigation of the sociological significance of
what we called paradigmatic experiences. On the level of
approach on which the pragmatist usually takes up the discussion, individuals and groups could survive if they only made the
right, that is to say, an efficient, adjustment to the ever-changing
world. Deeper analysis showed that a society based upon the
practice of efficient adjustment alone would sooner or later end
up in disintegration: beginning with a disintegration of character
and conduct of its members, followed by complete paralysis in
the field of action, and ending up in a paralysis of co-operative
activities as the deeper purpose would vanish from its institutions.
It is very likely—as we pointed out—that the present apathy in
the most civilized societies is at least partly due to the evaporation
of the paradigmatic experiences, and perhaps to the weakening
of the primordial images which in the past lent meaning to
human action.

A further exploration of the nature of paradigmatic experiences showed that one part of them goes back to the most
ancient sources of history. They preserve primordial images,

which emanate from the archaic depth of the mind. These archetypes work through religious tradition, and in the past did not only integrate human personality but also the social pattern. If the social climate is one of general conventionalization, there will be a tendency in them towards ossification. But even in this state there is a latent power in them, which may become virulent whenever the life of society becomes dynamic. Sudden outbursts, an unexpected re-activation of the underlying vision, are always possible. Much more exploration is wanted for the understanding of the nature of the Humanitarian and the Communist type of paradigmatic experiences. One can immediately sense that they are ultimately also archaic in origin. But their historical transformation is different in nature from those which were handed down to this age in religious traditions. There are more elements of rationality in them. And in this sense they are better adapted to the prevailing trend, the growth of the Ratio, but they also share the fate of Ratio. This fate seems to be that in its early phases it is dynamic, synthetic, full of utopian tension, but as soon as life gets more settled, security develops, division of labour along rational and functional lines grows, the analytic aspects of the very same Ratio become dominant. This may still produce many most valuable results, yet the pattern of analytic thinking once turned into a method of living disrupts rather than integrates human relations.

It follows from the distinction between adjustment character and paradigmatic vision in Christian action that, on the one hand, there is an obligation on the Christian to be conservative in so far as the essence of Christian experience of life goes, and, on the other hand, to be very progressive as far as the understanding of changes in the modern world are concerned.

It is not contradictory to be moved by an ancient vision as the basic experience of life and to understand the needs and potentialities of a new situation. The first gives direction to all action—the latter makes for presentness and prevents us from becoming absentees from the historical process.

(9) *The Emerging Social Pattern in its Economic Aspects*

If this historical absenteeism is to be avoided, one of the main concerns of Christian thinking at the present juncture is to decide which among the alternatives of social reconstruction are most compatible with the basic vision of life that has been experienced as Christian. By stating the case in this way it is admitted that neither the Christians nor any other group have the power to shape society entirely according to their vision. There are two or three emerging patterns of social organization from which one has to choose. Or, since they are not ready-made patterns but rather dynamic tendencies, it would be more correct to say: One has to side with that tendency which promises to create the widest scope for a type of life which is nearest to one's vision. It is the contention of this enquiry that the emerging pattern of "Planning for Freedom" is based upon a vision of society which in itself is not necessarily Christian but which creates the conditions under which Christian life is possible in modern society. The pattern is timely in so far as it realizes the need for a planned society. It does not, however, eliminate freedom but rather plans the scope for it. Society, as this pattern envisages it, is planned, yet its planning is democratically agreed, although the meaning of Democracy in an age of mass society will have to be revised, thought out anew in many respects, and adapted to the novel conditions.

Communists and Fascists also plan society, but they destroy the values of Western civilization and abolish Freedom, Democracy and respect for Personality. In contrast to this solution, the democratic form of planning will do everything to make planning compatible with these values. It would be misleading and dishonest to pretend that the Third Way, the pattern of "Planning for Freedom," exists as a blue print. But then neither Communism nor Fascism started with ready-made plans. It can, however, be said that at different places and in the different branches of human activity thinking men are at work who are groping towards that Third Way, in economics, active politics, political science, sociology, education, etc. Often they may not even be aware of the others' labours and contributions. It is therefore an urgent need that as many as possible of these should be brought together and their isolated activities correlated through an integrating vision of the pattern as a whole.

At the moment, effort is needed to elaborate even more clearly the principles in which the pattern of democratic planning differs from the totalitarian forms. It is equally urgent fully to study how the scheme would apply those principles in concrete life. If, e.g., one watches the trend of economic thought, one can easily detect different tendencies at work which more or less consciously move in one direction. The thoughts of those experts, theoretical and practical men, ought to be confronted, who realize that in the future a mastery of the keyboard of planned economy is necessary and inevitable, but who are equally keen on preserving scope for initiative wherever it is compatible with the general plan. This kind of focussing and confrontation of thought is extremely urgent, and the necessary differences and shades of opinion which will appear ought not to make us shirk the responsibility. We might, for instance, find that some thinkers will strive to modify as little as possible in the traditional system of market economy and insert measures of central control only where it is absolutely necessary in order to allay the devastating effects of the trade cycle. Others may believe that planning requires deeper inroads to be made into the economic and social structure. It certainly will do no harm to express differences like these quite openly and without restraint, as long as they help us to see what each solution costs in terms of additional regulations and to make quite sure that nobody will regulate for the sake of regulation, an attitude which is certainly not quite foreign to the engineer's type of mind so much in the foreground in our age. If the existing differences of opinion and conviction were fully thrashed out, we should at least know on which issues it is worth differing. Thus fortified, we should not drift blindly into totalitarian regimentation, which must devour everything we call Freedom.

Or, to mention another vital aspect: our economists, who are resolved to plan for freedom and not for total regimentation outright, should tell us which classes and groups will profit, which will lose most, if one scheme or the other is carried out. We are aware that Planning for Freedom has its price, and we have to be willing to pay heavily for it if it proves the only way to maintain human conditions of life and is not to be paid for by murder, concentration camps and the suspension of all liberties which make life worth living. If we know who will suffer most from any necessary alterations, it is possible to provide for them, to compensate them, to re-train them, to give them new functions in society. As long as the *cui bono* of a system is kept dark it can only cause anxieties which will ruin us all.

Apart from the various interests affected by the new system, there is also a moral price to be paid for a new order. We hear much about moral regeneration, about the substitution of the profit motive by the idea of service. Christian realism will have to ask very concrete questions of the economists who envisage a structure which maintains parts of our present economic system and removes other harmful ones. They, in co-operation with the sociologists, will have to answer the question whether the emerging society can do without the profit motive, and in which parts of the existing system it is already beginning to disappear, in which it is still irreplaceable, and also where it can be replaced or supplemented by the motive of service or by psychological incentives not yet sufficiently clearly described.

Of course, we must come to a co-operation of all concerned, not only for the discussion of economic problems. Nothing but such co-operation can enable us to discuss the problem of personal responsibility, not only in the abstract, which is an unsatisfactory method of discussion, but also with reference to social opportunity. For instance, it is no use talking of increasing private initiative and responsibility when the general trend in business life and elsewhere is to turn the many small entrepreneurs into employees or bureaucrats. A solution can only be found when one knows exactly what are the strategic points in the economic and the social structure, where deterioration is setting in and where new opportunities for initiative and personal responsibility are emerging. Such an approach translates the inarticulate craving for greater freedom, initiative and responsibility into concrete practical problems, which can be solved by experience and by consulting practical men. The elaboration of these opportunities for different attitudes is important for our educational policy. It is obvious that education for competitiveness is no use, if the coming order does not, or should not, rely upon competitive attitudes. There is no point in inculcating attitudes of absolute pacifism and non-resistance, if for a long time to come the world is a militant one. At any rate, the propagation of the pacifist attitude can honestly be pursued only if we have the courage to face all the conditions under which these special ideas can be put into practice in our world.

(10) *The Emerging Social Pattern and the Problem of Power and Social Control*

It is not only the economic structure which defines the scope of future patterns of behaviour, but also the political and social structure of a society. Thus we shall have to study what forms of power will or should exist, and how power should be distributed and controlled. We must approach these urgent questions in a realistic, i.e. neither in a utopian nor in a reactionary fashion. Society to us cannot be a community of angels, a social system which could function without pressure of any kind and which could base everything upon absolute, spontaneous consensus. Instead of being realistic this is the approach of anarchistic utopianism, an approach which denies the need for power altogether and which imagines it possible to build society on the basis of mutual aid, co-operation and love alone. The opposite approach is equally unsatisfactory and falls short of reality. This, the reactionary, attitude more or less complacently accepts the existing forms of social and political oppression as eternal ones and does not seek to change the social techniques in use. The reactionary approach thus precludes a philosophy of power which ultimately believes only in the effectiveness of naked power and tends to substitute the techniques of pressure and command for all other social techniques, as supremely realized in the philosophy and practice of the Nazis. But we cannot accept the philosophy of power prevailing in commercial society either which is ready to think that all evils resulting from power are absent if only the use of naked power can be avoided, but which does not mind pressure which often achieves the desired effect by economic or other indirect methods, such as exclusive clique systems, monopolistic and other vested interests, or the exploitation of educational opportunities for the benefit of one particular, privileged class.

Here again a general discussion of the legitimate forms of the use of power will become relevant only if these general ideas are followed up in the sphere of concrete application to the social order of the future. Just as we expect the expert economist to outline the picture of our type of planned economy so as to enable us approximately at least to fit in the psychological and moral corollaries, the political scientist ought to describe concrete forms of the use of power as they will be required in an order which is both planned and democratically controlled.

To ask for such a picture, in which the economic and power structure is depicted in a strict correlation with the psychological attitudes and moral standards which go with it, is not asking for the impossible. It is only very much against our traditional thought-habits, in which psychology and social structure are kept in separate watertight compartments. If it is possible, provided you know the rules of the game, such as football, cricket, chess, etc., to tell which of them will foster co-operation, which individual competition, team spirit or unbridled aggressiveness, etc., it should also be possible to foretell with a certain amount of probability which kind of virtues and psychological attitudes are required to make a democratic society work, and how far planning will complicate the pattern.

If the changing power structure is described in broad outlines, the kind of discipline which will have to prevail in it on different occasions can also be foreseen, and equally its pedagogical aspects, as, e.g., what kind of training is apt to produce the discipline required. It is very likely that a democratically controlled planned society will be mainly based upon a new kind of self-control, where people stop arguing about differences when it comes to action and decision. Spontaneously they consent on submitting to a kind of temporary dictator in themselves, if otherwise the superimposition of a dictator from without would be the only solution. This type of democratic self-discipline can only be achieved if secular and religious education, the press and other factors in public opinion, voluntarily co-operate. It is not impossible to sketch the outlines of such a synthetic picture of a new social order, detailed enough to give lead to a new social and educational policy.

If we fail to replace the vanishing old social controls by new ones, we can be quite sure that substitute controls will emerge, but it is very doubtful that these haphazardly emerging new controls will be more adequate than those which could be provided by the co-operative thinking of the best brains among our scientists, theologians, philosophers, educationists, social workers, etc. If in our mass society neither the school nor the church and religion provide codes, patterns of action and paradigmatic experiences, it is the cinema and other commercialized institutions which take over the rôle of teaching people what to strive for, whom to obey, how to be free, how to love.

If elaborating a vision for the future, such as the hammering out of an educational policy which corresponds to the nature of a society with our concept of freedom, power and authority, seems too difficult a task for our best thinkers, no doubt there will be others less scrupulous who will do the job for them.

(11) *The Nature of the Co-operative Effort that is wanted if the Transition from an Unplanned to a Planned Society is to be understood*

It will be obvious by now that it is not with the idea of re-directing theology, sociology and education in terms of a blue print that I should solicit from the economist and sociologist a provisional scheme for the workable social order at which we are aiming, nor with the intention of creating a utopian image and taking its realization for granted. It is simply that no reorientation is possible at the present juncture without first discussing the principles which should guide us. Yet even being clear about the eventual direction does not mean that we are not bound to start from the world as it is, nor that planning the transition is not at least as important as planning the subsequent stage. For many reasons, therefore, it will be important to get reliable information from the economist and the political scientist concerning those changes in the direction of planning which have occurred during the present war. Although many of these regulations and techniques of planning will disappear after the war, some of them are the jumping-off ground for peace-time planning. It is therefore very important to decide with expert help which types of interference if freely developed lead to Fascism, and which can be utilized as stepping-stones towards the order we desire.

The idea that planning the transition is even more important than planning the ensuing stage carries with it the suggestion that it is healthy to start by analysing those deficiencies which we find unbearable in our present society. The revolt against evils in our society often contains in itself the creative, constructive and positive suggestion. Thus concrete criticism of the present educational system, of the neglect of Youth and of the evils of unemployment, will contribute in itself to an organic transition of society. Of course, if these reformist attacks remain isolated and there is no will to see the interdependence between the symptoms, then I do not see how a remedy can be found at the present stage of development. Without aiming at an integrated picture of the whole of society we cannot efficiently cope with the difficulties. It is here that the theologian, the philosopher and the sociologist, whose job it is to think about man and his life in society, can supplement the work of the Civil Servant and the social worker, who are accustomed professionally to think in terms of isolated symptoms and departments.

While it is healthy to start with the concrete attack, it will perhaps be a useful warning that in dealing with maladjustments in modern society one should always bear in mind the fact that they are mostly the outcome of the Capitalist system or of urbanization or of mechanization. This distinction is important, as the remedy for each of these evils is to be sought in different devices, and one is often inclined to attribute to Capitalism evils which are caused by urbanization or by mechanization. When dealing with the problem of leisure, for example, these three evils have to be treated separately.

Another very fundamental social aspect which is crucial for the translation of Christian principles into modern conditions is that Christian values were originally expressed in terms of a neighbourhood community in an agrarian world. They are virtues of a primary group (Cooley).[11] That is to say, they are virtues which directly apply to conditions where personal contacts prevail. In primary groups the commandment "Love your neighbour" is not paradoxical, whereas it is at least not immediately evident how one should follow this commandment in Great Society where you do not even know the members personally, let alone love them, which is a personal attitude *par excellence*. Now Christianity is built upon this paradox. Its novelty consists in expanding the primary group virtues on to the enlarged environment of the world. It makes the principle of neighbourhood relationships the principle of large-scale social organization. The paradox cannot be solved on the level of the naïve and unsophisticated mind which is inclined immediately to apply this attitude to everyone and everything. The real solution can only be found by projecting the essence of the paradigma on to a different social plane. In the world of large-scale institutions this means tolerating only those institutions which either embody in their structure the principles of these primary virtues, or make it possible for these virtues to be practised in personal relationships. For instance, democracy as a political institution is a projection on to the organizational plane of the principle of brotherhood, everyone being equal at least in political rights and opportunities. To illustrate how institutions may prevent the development of personal relationships in the Christian spirit, Tolstoy once pointed out that the institution of serfdom was un-Christian because from the very outset it prevented the possibility of Christian brotherhood both in the conduct of the serf and of the overlord. Of course, in a fuller discussion of the problem it could be said that there is always scope outside institutions for practising the essential commandments of Christianity in personal relationships. For instance, the overlord and the serf, inspired by the example of Christ, could still break through established social and political relationships and behave as Christians. This may certainly be true and practicable to a large extent, and it is the duty of Christians to emphasize that Christianity must primarily be practised in the personal sphere and that there are things which are not dependent on political factors. Yet it is highly dangerous if this experience is upheld as a pretext and an excuse for acquiescence, indolence and subservience in politics proper. At all times it has been difficult to keep personal relationships apart from the surrounding social and political structure. And this becomes increasingly difficult in the modern world, where the tendency towards totalitarianism is opposed to establishing oases of privacy and purely personal relationships.[12]

The spirit of a social system cannot, as a rule, be immediately assessed, but actually it permeates everything. Its negative effects can only be judged by following up the implications of the whole mental atmosphere that goes with them. Thus, for instance, the limitations of the Greek way of life only become apparent when one remembers how Aristotle took it for granted that slaves were subhuman. An example like this makes the impossibility of escaping from politics evident.

(12) *Analysis of some Concrete Issues which are subject to Re-valuation*

After this detailed discussion of the implications of a re-interpretation of Christian valuations, I am now turning to the analysis of values themselves.

I pointed out at the beginning of the discussion [13] that a reinterpretation of valuations which are inherent in a tradition can only be carried out in group work, for the values themselves are only present in shared experience. It is, therefore, left to such groups to fulfil the task properly. What I can do now is to select some examples which show that the re-valuation is in the making and to point out approximately what the task would be. Only group work could show how much disagreement exists between those who were brought up and live within an identical tradition and those who do not share such a background; also how far these different traditional attitudes are challenged by the new situation, how far they have developed new responses, and how much agreement on the new situation could be brought about by democratic discussion. If such group work were to succeed, its work itself would contribute a great deal to the problem of whether democratic guidance on value issues in a changing and mixed society is feasible.

I propose to discuss the whole range of valuations under three main headings, without claiming that this classification is final:

(1) General Ethics.
(2) Ethics of personal relationships.
(3) Ethics of organized relationships.

For each of these spheres I shall mention one problem, which stands as an example for many others.

Under the heading of "General Ethics" there should be grouped all those valuations which regulate human behaviour in general, that is to say, irrespective of the specific type of relationship in which it occurs. They mostly follow from our vision of human dignity or from whatever we may consider as essential in human beings.

As contrasted with the sphere of General Ethics we have to consider those valuations which regulate human behaviour in specific relationships, that is to say, either in personal or in organized relationships.

In our educational approach, for instance, we take care of the first sphere when we impart the ideal of the gentleman, that is, attitudes which should prevail everywhere. We cater for the sphere of personal relationships when speaking about the legitimate demands of a wife or a friend on our behaviour; and for the sphere of organized relationships when we define the right behaviour of an employer toward his employees or vice versa.

It is in this latter sphere of businesslike, organized relationships that a complete revolution is going on and that, as far as I can see, the Churches have not yet consistently developed their point of view. To appreciate the significance of this sphere one has only to think of the fact that the dignity of a man's personality does not only develop within the sphere of personal relationships but is equally fostered or hampered in organized relationships.

I. *General Ethics*

(*a*) The Problem of Survival Values

As the best example of the dilemma of our times in this sphere I suggest the analysis of "survival values." By " survival values" I understand those values which characterize all activities with the purpose of guaranteeing or safeguarding the survival of the individual or the group. We owe it to the challenge of Nazism that this problem holds the centre of our attention. Whereas in their philosophy there exists, so to speak, no other values than those serving the survival of a "race" or "Volk," to us the problem is where to place these survival values in the hierarchy of values. We cannot, of course, completely discard them, though the ascetic tendencies in Christianity sometimes tried to disparage them. The struggle in our time between the survival values and higher issues such as freedom or faith can best be expressed by well-known maxims such as : "Primum vivere dein philosophari," "Navigare necesse est, vivere non est necesse," although the latter statement can be explained not only as a clash between values of a higher order and survival values, but also as one between the demands of individual and group survival. The group needed navigation, and in comparison with that need the individual's claim for survival was considered inferior.

In the present situation this clash between survival values and some higher purpose often takes the form of a conflict between

efficiency and a democratic solution. For example, in certain
cases planning based upon compulsion and subservience may
bring quicker results than planning that appeals to voluntary
co-operation and consultation of the community. In its most
acute form we may then be faced with a dilemma which can be
formulated as follows: "What is the good of democracy if we
do not survive?" or alternatively, "What is the good of surviving
if we lose our freedom?"

This issue becomes more urgent than ever before in an age of
large-scale organization. Formerly, in the age of handicrafts and
community life, the lack of efficiency in one decision could be
compensated for in other fields. Now we may have to choose
between comprehensive issues such as compulsory rationing and
voluntary savings, or between conscription and military service
on a voluntary basis. In both cases the wrong decision carries
gigantic consequences which cannot be offset without further
compensating efforts, for if one fails to introduce rationing in
time one may lose the war altogether. Inefficiency in this field
then directly affects survival. Thus we have first to make the
primary choice in our hierarchy between the survival value of
efficiency and democracy. Once this is settled we can turn to
concrete issues and work out the casuistry of individual decisions.

It will be the specific task of theologians or of the type of
groups which I mentioned to work out that casuistry and present
it to the public in the form of recommendations. In a democratic
society there is no need to dictate valuations, but this advice and
guidance is wanted, for it is hardly possible for the average citizen
to judge the merits of a case in such a highly complex society
as ours.

Of course only in marginal cases is there an absolute choice
between efficiency and democracy, for very often the result of a
careful investigation will be to discover as yet unexplored democratic ways of being efficient. It also becomes clear that the
efficiency principle is more or less relevant according to the nature
of the different tasks; for example, in transport, efficiency
measurable in terms of time and costs may be absolutely predominant, whereas the efficiency of educational institutions
measured in costs, etc., may be of secondary importance. Careful investigation also shows that the term "efficiency" is mostly
ambiguous, since no assessment of efficiency is possible without

first asking, "Efficiency for what?" For instance, a rigid taxation measure may be very efficient in extracting the maximum sum from the taxpayer at a given moment, but it may at the same time destroy his solvency and impair his future ability to pay taxes. Or again, inflation may extract the savings of certain classes but for ever destroy their will to save.

(b) The Problem of Asceticism

A real revolution in the general evaluation of survival values is going on with regard to efficiency as well as in connection with everything that contributes to health and vitality. The latter is a part of that anti-ascetic trend prevailing all over the world with which especially the Protestant tradition is faced. There will be no difficulty in attributing value to everything that fosters health and vitality, but how the Puritan tradition will react to the removal of taboos on various forms and degrees of self-expression is another matter. Here the ascetic tendencies of Calvinism still prevail, and it is a question of how far they were temporary and historical and how far they are essential for Christianity at large. In such a discussion distinction ought to be made between various forms of ascetic attitudes and their merits and demerits, and one ought to decide whether Max Weber and others are correct in stating as a result of their investigations that the asceticist "saving" attitude of the Puritans was a preliminary to the growth of the Capitalist spirit. It is not impossible to hold the view that this taboo on self-expression in most spheres of life, sociologically speaking, corresponded to the phase of "primary accumulation" in the early stages of Capitalism. The small artisan could only become an entrepreneur if he was ready to sacrifice immediate pleasure for future use by accumulating his savings instead of consuming his surplus. But the saving attitude in one field could only be established if the discipline which goes with it was extended to every sphere of life. It is clear that in this case asceticism became a social discipline which influenced working and consuming habits, thought and character patterns and the meaning and rôle of culture and leisure.

In this discussion we shall have to listen carefully to those who regard this type of asceticism only as one aspect of a psychology of scarcity which in many ways is no longer in keeping with the times. It is out of date because we are living in an age of potential plenty and the fears which drive us into wars are ultimately remnants of a world where starvation was always lurking around the corner. According to this view, obsolete attitudes of asceticism prevent us from organizing the world along reasonable lines where there would be enough to go round and everybody could get his proper share.

However, on the other side, we must equally listen to those who point to the fact that our limitless craving for more and more luxury goods, when it penetrates even to the lowest classes, is the unnatural response to endless stimulation of desires originating in a competitive system, where the producers try to outdo each other by creating cravings for new kinds of goods. As a reaction against that endless stimulation a movement could be fostered which is based upon the view that moderation and restriction are essential for the human being.

I do not wish to make any decision in this controversy. But one has to ask: Which are the permanent and which the lasting values of asceticism, and where does our age reveal new aspects of it? It is, once more, the task of ministers, social workers and doctors to tell us how these norms of asceticism work out in actual life, what sort of conflicts they cause in individual and social relationships and, especially, what sort of conflicts arise when these ascetic evaluations disappear without being replaced by other values and principles.

(c) The Split Consciousness

In the discussion of survival values a general reminder may be of some use. Whether we like it or not, life is to a great extent a struggle for survival. Self-assertion is a part of it. In ethics there are roughly three ways of dealing with that fact. The first, which the Nazis have followed, is to make this principle *the* principle of human conduct. This in itself leads to barbarism. The second is the opposite principle, i.e. the complete denial of the moral right, of the existence of these self-assertive tendencies. This attitude often leads to hypocrisy, as a certain amount of self-assertion and egotism are necessary for survival, and if our moral consciousness will not admit this, then they will have to be left to develop by means of a split consciousness. In my view, the third way is to aim not at the entire suppression of the self-asserting attitudes but at their conscious control, which means that we admit them to the extent that they are necessary for the survival of the individual or the group, as the case may be, but that at the same time we consciously keep watch that these boundaries are not passed. Of course, this kind of control is only possible if at the same time we develop our powers of awareness. The more we study modern society, the clearer it will become that without a deliberate increase in that awareness in education the democratic way of life cannot survive. It is not wholly impossible that the repressive attitude towards self-expression was due in the past to the impossibility of creating at short notice the rational powers needed for self-control, and so instead the method of putting a taboo on self-expression became the general device.

II. *Ethics of Personal Relationships*

(*a*) The Problem of Privacy in the Modern World

In this sphere I should like to discuss as one of the changing attitudes the gradual fading out of the meaning of privacy and the emergence of the habit of mass enjoyment and the tendency towards mass ecstasy. By choosing this example I do not want to belittle the deplorable effects of the weakening of shared experiences in small groups and the evaporation of meaning from communal activities. They have frequently been discussed, whereas the problem of privacy versus mass ecstasy needs further exploration.

By privacy and inwardness we understand the desire of the individual to withdraw certain inner experiences from the control of the outer world and to claim them for himself. Privacy and inwardness are perhaps the strongest means of individualization and one of the greatest assets in the growth of an independent personality. It is in this realm of seclusion and partial isolation that our experiences gain in depth and that we become spiritually different from our fellow-men. In those spheres where we are continually exposed to social contacts and where an exchange of ideas incessantly takes place, we tend to become like each other through mutual adjustment. This process of socializing our experiences is a healthy one as long as it is balanced by a sphere of privacy. Without it there is no power left in the self to resist

continual change and the individual develops into a bundle of
unco-ordinated patterns of adjustment.

It is not only the individual who needs this sphere of seclusion
and mental privacy into which he can always withdraw and
cultivate traits of his personal differentiation as the most valuable
parts of the self. Dynamic society itself cannot cope with the
great variety of problems as they emerge from the ever-changing
scene without drawing upon a great reservoir of individuals who
have developed beyond conformity, and who are always apt to
produce unexpected responses when traditional forms of adjustment become obsolete. It is no wonder, then, that primitive
societies did not know the phenomenon of privacy, and that even
in a village of our own time one can hardly make a clear distinction between home and public affairs. As in a village
neighbourly help is essential, one's door is, so to speak, always
open and public control penetrates into every hidden nook of
family and individual life.

It is perhaps no exaggeration to say that the sources of our
modern desire for privacy are to be found in the gradual emergence of the bourgeoisie. It was in the world of industry and
commerce that for the first time the workshop and office became
separated from the home, and as the merchants grew richer it
became possible for members of the family to have a room of
their own, thus setting up the external framework for the differentiation of our attitudes and feelings into private and public.

England was the country in which this cult of privacy was
most fully developed, so that solitude became a virtue desired
not only by the bourgeoisie but by all social strata. No doubt it
is due to Protestantism that religion became a private relationship
between the soul and God. The exclusion of the mediating
services of the Church between man's conscience and God is
just another expression of the very same process of making the
most significant experiences the exclusive possession of the person.
Early mediaeval Catholicism corresponds to an agrarian world
in which primary tribal cohesion is still strong and community
feeling so intense that the climax of human experience can be
reached in communal experience. The Holy Mass is the spiritualized expression of group ecstasy and the ancient striving for the
fusion of souls, and it is only by a gradual process that the whole
performance becomes symbolical to most of the worshippers.

The idea of having one's deepest experiences in public without profaning them becomes strange to the world of the bourgeois, in which not only ecstasy but any deeper emotion is a personal and private affair.

The monks were the first people in the mediaeval world who not only realized the significance of the inwardness which flourishes in privacy, but planned the environment in which it would grow. They mastered the art of social isolation. Total and partial isolation combined with work, prayers and psychological exercises produced a mental state which would never occur in the world of affairs. Contemplation, spiritualization, sublimation and religious ecstasy became an art and the privileged possession of a new kind of specialist. Thus an élite of inwardness was deliberately created—a new nobility or caste system in which those were considered leaders who advanced furthest along the path of inner experience, shared only by a few, and not those who showed the greatest skill in worldly adjustment. This pride in inwardness, privacy and asceticism cultivated by the monks was, so to speak, secularized by the Protestants,[14] who expected their leaders to show the virtues of asceticism, inwardness and self-discipline.

Thus the tradition of privacy and inwardness was religious and at the same time closely linked up with the urban environment. As long as handicrafts prevailed, the social conditions under which they were carried on only added to the dissemination of the same mental attitude. Working in small workshops, very often alone, encouraged contemplation and day-dreaming. It was no mere chance that Jacob Böhme the mystic was a cobbler, and that religious sects spread among artisans.

These pre-conditions favourable to privacy and contemplation were first threatened by the Industrial Revolution with its big factories, mechanical work and the growth of big cities with their crowding, mass amusements, mass excitement and political demonstrations. The existence of intimacy, privacy, contemplation and inwardness is threatened wherever modern mass society develops, whether here or in America, Germany or Russia. Despite political differences the very same trait prevails. The sense of privacy and contemplation is supplanted by a striving for movement, excitement and group ecstasy. André Gide, in his *Back from the U.S.S.R.*, writes: "The kolkhosian takes all his pleasures in common. His room is merely a place to sleep in; the whole interest of his life has passed into his club, his park of culture, his various meeting-places. What more can be desired? The happiness of all can only be obtained by disindividualizing each. The happiness of all can only be obtained at the expense of each. In order to be happy, conform."

If England and France do not yet show these new features completely, it is only on account of the fact that the bourgeois background is still strong enough to keep the balance against the growing influence of mass existence. The department stores and factories cater for people who are fed on mass entertainments such as the cinema and the dance-hall, who thus acquire habits of mind to which in politics the mass meeting with its excitement and group ecstasy corresponds. In the midst of an advanced civilization we are reaching a stage which reinstates group attitudes that formerly belonged to primitive ecstatic religions. Was not Judaism determined by its struggle against the ecstatic magic of the agricultural god Baal and against the fertility orgies of his priests? The more ascetic and rational attitude of the Jewish tradition was later accepted by Christianity, in which only a few remnants of this magical attitude survived, to be later expurgated by Protestantism.

(b) The Problem of Mass Ecstasy

It is against this background that we have to discuss the merits and demerits of privacy and inwardness on the one hand and the meaning of the re-emergence of the symptoms of mass hysteria and ecstasy on the other. In the first place, we shall have to make a clear distinction between the various forms of privacy and inwardness, and shall have to decide in which cases their survival seems to be of real significance. But we shall equally have to remember that the existence of the attitude of contemplation and a sense of privacy does not only depend upon our desires, but that there are certain social conditions which foster or hamper their development. Only with reference to these conditions is some kind of spiritual strategy conceivable in the future. The idea of strategy indicates that we must not take all the negative tendencies of modern society for granted nor look upon the achievements of a long tradition of privacy and inwardness as doomed. On the contrary, a thorough knowledge of the social factors which support the mental habits we value will help us to save them for future generations.

As regards the modern movements of mass ecstasy, an entirely negative policy towards them would be futile. It is unlikely that there should be no positive values compatible with such unifying emotions on a large scale. They represent a kind of shared experience, and the proper question to ask is whether their spiritualization instead of sheer emotionalization would be feasible. After all, a Cathedral Mass is also a spiritualized collective ecstatic experience. The problem, therefore, is rather to find new forms of spiritualization than completely to deny the potentialities inherent in the new forms of group existence.[15]

III. *Ethics of Organized Relationships*

Since in our society work and recreation, production and consumption, mostly rest upon large-scale organization, it is obvious that this will have a considerable impact upon our behaviour and conduct and their evaluation. As far as primary, purely personal relationships are concerned, we can assume that they will take care of themselves, and advice and guidance will mainly be needed when things go wrong. In the sphere of organized relationships, on the other hand, the organizer creates the relationship, and we can hardly expect anything satisfactory to emerge without a great deal of social awareness, knowledge and moral sense. The psychological and moral crisis of our time is to a large extent due to the speed with which the industrial revolution built up its new organization, hardly leaving time to realize the psychological and moral implications of the changes it brought about. It has for long been obvious to the sociologist that if there is a clash between the principles of organization and the psychological needs of the individual, and if institutions do not succeed in enlisting the souls of men employed in them, then their emotions go sour and general restlessness prevents constructive development.

In the realm of large-scale organization I find it even more difficult than elsewhere to show a single example which could illustrate the rest of the problem. This difficulty is due to the fact that in the world of organized relationships, more than in other fields, the new ethics is not confined to any one phase of the whole social process but permeates the whole pattern which co-ordinates the contributions of the individuals who partake in it. Here more than elsewhere there are no virtues in isolation, but all emerge out of the new spirit in which a factory, a school or a service are organized. Instead of giving an isolated piece of experience, an isolated problem of moral casuistry, I shall therefore try here rather to show how the different emerging moral issues in a modern factory depend on one another and on the nature and spirit of the whole organization.

What in future can be done in these fields depends partly on the objective nature of the organized relationships in a factory, that is, on the needs they have to satisfy, and partly on those promising tendencies of the new age which try to answer these needs in a novel way. It is in the realm of the latter that Christians have to judge for themselves how far these tendencies correspond to the basic experience we call Christian. As to the needs first mentioned, we can only judge re-valuations in the sphere of organized relationships, in our case a factory, if we thoroughly understand the basic needs the new morality tries to satisfy. These fundamental needs are of a twofold nature: (1) they have to guarantee an objective and efficient working order; (2) they have to satisfy the psychological needs of the individual.[16]

Quite tentatively I enumerate some of the needs to which every ethic of organized relationships has to answer with reference to a factory, for instance. Every organized relationship has its:

(1) Sanctions—varying from corporal punishment to fines, moral condemnation, etc.
(2) Discipline—time-table, working habits, etc.
(3) Code of Conduct—behaviour towards co-workers, foreman, etc.
(4) Assignment of Responsibility—individual and collective.
(5) Working Incentives and Rewards—bonuses, enjoyment of one's technical skill, desire for recognition, etc.
(6) Intellectual Appreciation of the Purpose of the Work—more or less relevant according to the social system we live in.
(7) Social Prestige of the Job.
(8) Social Hierarchy within the Factory.
Etc.

These are all phases in a system of evaluation, and any attempt at re-valuation must deal carefully with each of them. It has to answer the need for collective efficiency and also to create moral and psychological gratification for those who are engaged in the work.

It is important to notice that both collective efficiency and psychological gratification can be secured by different systems, and the transition from one age to another consists in passing from one technique of social gratification and ethical valuation to another (transmutation of social techniques and of their value aspects).[17]

This is where the problem of the New Spirit comes in. We cannot create it. Only if it is already at work can we strengthen those tendencies in it which we desire to prevail. I can only very tentatively give my personal diagnosis of those new trends which are relevant from our point of view. There is on the one hand a tendency towards authoritarianism permeating all our organized relationships. There is a tendency to introduce into the sphere of work the military pattern of command and blind obedience. On the other hand, there are often very strong tendencies at work beneath the surface, which are at the same time anti-Fascist, anti-Communist and anti-Capitalist, representing fundamentally new strivings of men and women. They do not yet form a new system, or a coherent outlook, but it is possible to point to these trends which, particularly under the revolutionizing effect of war, are emerging here and there irrespective of the political organization which prevails.

(1) There is a general re-valuation emerging in the economic organization at large, which moves from purely financial calculation towards thinking in terms of "organic welfare."[18] As Ruskin put it: "There is no wealth but life." The war itself compelled us to discard money calculations and to consider as real wealth natural resources and man-power. The calculation in terms of private costs (e.g. how much is spent on wages by a firm) is gradually being replaced by a calculation in terms of "social costs" (e.g. how much is spent on unemployment by the community at large).

(2) Parallel with it in the sphere of working incentives is a move from purely financial recompense to the motive of Service. With it goes a greater desire for recognition of

self-realization through work, a craving for more purposeful work.

(3) As to some basic psychological needs, there is a move away from a world in which either the rentier's exaggerated craving for security or the adventurousness of the entrepreneur and speculator prevailed, towards an integrated attitude in which security for everybody as regards elementary basic needs should be combined with collective venture in the social and cultural fields.

(4) There is also a movement away from a concept of freedom modelled on the activity of financial investment and speculation towards those forms of freedom which seek for creativeness in other fields of life as well. A campaign of slum-clearance, the creation of settlements and educational advance, call for at least as much initiative and inventiveness as independent economic enterprises.

(5) Finally, there is a move towards a true democracy arising from dissatisfaction with the infinitesimal contribution guaranteed by universal suffrage, a democracy which through careful decentralization of functions allots a creative social task to everyone. The same fundamental democratization claims for everyone a share in real education, one which no longer seeks primarily to satisfy the craving for social distinction, but enables us adequately to understand the pattern of life in which we are called upon to live and act.

These trends partly overlap and partly cut across the tendencies that are present in the existing systems. They are too democratic to develop adequately in totalitarian systems, and they are too much beyond the horizon of the Economic Man of the passing era to develop fully within the framework of an unplanned democracy.

Under present circumstances these tendencies will not necessarily win through, but they are healthy tendencies fermenting underneath the surface, and those who aim at Planning for Freedom should do everything in their power to strengthen them. There is a reasonable chance that after the war the struggle between antagonistic dogmatic systems will have burnt out and there will be a desire to develop potentialities which at present can only be diagnosed as latent tendencies of a Third Way.

I am aware of the fact that an over-emphasis on the humanization of organized relationships in factory, Civil Service and elsewhere, without reorganizing the economic structure in its fundamentals, might be misused by those who only want to alter human relationships on the surface without paying the price of structural reconstruction. But the only remedy for this possible misuse is social awareness. Just as it is impossible in the long run to humanize leisure and factory relationships within a dictatorial system, where the pattern of command and obedience will necessarily break through everywhere, so it is equally impossible to humanize factory relationships as long as the basis of calculation remains efficiency in terms of money returns and profits instead of social welfare.

[NOTES

NOTES TO CHAPTER I

[1] In this book, the terms " laissez-faire " and " Liberalism " are used as ideal types, i.e. the term does not exactly designate reality as it is or ever was, but it deliberately emphasizes certain features which are relevant for the purposes of the presentation and for the valuations prevailing in the latter. Without focussing on such ideal types for developing clear-cut antinomies, it would be impossible to make one's points in a political discussion.

On the other hand, justice to the source from which we draw so much of our sustenance is restored, if we remind the reader that Liberalism, neither in its philosophy nor in its practice, ever completely corresponded to what could be called pure laissez-faire, that is to say the belief that self-adjustment both in the economic field and in the other spheres of social activity spontaneously leads to an equilibrium. Especially classical English Liberalism never demanded the complete absence of controls.

Nevertheless, after these reservations have been made it is still true that the laissez-faire ideology hoped for something like spontaneous self-adjustment, and in its exaggerated form it was partly responsible for the disintegration of communal controls in the later phases of capitalist Democracy in the course of which not equilibrium but crises and monopolies developed.

[2] Cf. my *Man and Society in an Age of Reconstruction : Studies in Modern Social Structure* (3rd ed., London, 1942), especially part v. This chapter is a brief restatement and further development of that book, where the reader can find a more detailed treatment of many of the problems presented here. Furthermore, the author is working on a book, " Essentials of Democratic Planning," which will deal in a more systematic manner with the different aspects of planning.

[3] E. Durkheim, *On the Division of Labour in Society* (transl. by G. Simpson : New York, 1933).

NOTES TO CHAPTER II

[1] The concept of value underlying the present discussion is deliberately one-sided. It presents the sociological, functional approach. This does not exclude, but rather leaves room for, the other approaches. Among other things, we are not dealing with differences which refer to the inner quality of the various values but with the social function they fulfil. Any real appreciation of values is primarily concerned with their qualitative aspects. It is, however, definitely advisable not to start the discussion on the highest level, but rather to consider the simpler aspects.

The reader will notice that Chapters II and V of this book take the functional approach, and that in the last chapter, VII, this approach is occasionally transcended and the inner, qualitative appreciation of values comes within the scope of the analysis.

[2] Cf. to the whole passage the pioneer work of C. H. Cooley, *Social Organisation : A Study of the Larger Mind* (New York, 1909).

[3] R. H. Tawney, *The Acquisitive Society* (London, 1921). Relevant for the whole discussion of this paragraph is L. L. Bernard, " Conflict between Primary Group Attitudes and Derivative Group Ideals in Modern Society," in *American Journal of Sociology*, vol. 41.

[4] Chicago Commission on Race Relations, *The Negro in Chicago : A Study of Race Relation and a Race Riot* (Chicago, 1922).

Some more Readings on the Subject.

K. Young, " Primitive Social Norms in Present-Day Education," in *Social Forces*, June 5, 1927.

W. I. Thomas, " Persistence of Primary Group Norms in Modern Education," in *Contribution of Modern Science to Education.*

Th. Veblen, " Christian Morals and the Competitive System," in *International Journal of Ethics*, vol. 20, 1910.

——, " Cultural Incidence of the Machine Process," in his *Theory of Business Enterprise.*

F. Knight, " Religion and Ethics in Modern Civilization," in *The Journal of Liberal Religion*, vol. iii., no. 1.

R. A. Woods, " The Neighbourhood in Social Reconstruction," in *Publications of the American Sociological Society*, vol. viii., 1913.

Notes to Chapter III

[1] Cf. C. Luetkens, *Die deutsche Jugendbewegung : Ein soziologischer Versuch* (Frankfurt a. M., 1925).

[2] E. Y. Hartshorne, *German Youth and the Nazi Dream of Victory* (New York and Toronto, 1941).

[3] Most relevant to the discussion of the sociology of Adolescents are the articles by E. B. Reuter, M. Mead, R. G. Foster *et al.* on " Sociological Research in Adolescence," in *American Journal of Sociology*, July 1936. Cf. also M. Mead, *Coming of Age in Samoa* (New York, 1928) ; C. B. Zachry and M. C. Lighty, " Report on the Study of Adolescence of the Commission on Secondary School Curriculum," *Emotion and Conduct in Adolescence* (New York, 1940) ; P. Blos, *The Adolescent Personality* (New York) ; H. P. Rainey (ed.), *How Fares American Youth ?* (Washington, D.C.) ; F. Redl, " Emotion and Group Leadership," in *Psychiatry*, 1942 ; E. De A. Partridge, *Leadership among Adolescent Boys* (Bureau of Publications, Teachers College, Columbia University, New York, 1934). Of special interest are the Publications of the American Council of Education on Negro Adolescence : J. Dollard and A. Davies, *Children of Bondage* ; C. S. Johnson and F. Frazer, *Negro Youth at the Cross-roads* ; W. L. Warner, *et al.*, *Class and the Color Barrier* ; and the summary of these studies by E. L. Sutherland, *Class, Color and Personality.*

From English literature, cf. A. E. Morgan, *The Needs of Youth* (London, 1939) ; " The Young Adult in Wales," *Report of the South Wales Council of Social Service*, Cardiff ; J. M. Brew, *In the Service of Youth* (London, 1943) ; P. Jephcott, *Girls Growing Up* (London, 1943).

[4] In the rise of the Nazi Party this typical position of the adolescent was enhanced by the outsider position into which whole classes of the German population had been driven first by the inflation and then by the economic crisis of 1929. This can be understood as one of the reasons for the preponderance both of young age-groups within the Party membership and of those occupational groups which were hit hardest by the depression and foresaw little future for themselves under the old system. (Cf. Hans Gerth, " The Nazi Party : Its Leadership and Composition," in *American Journal of Sociology*, January 1941.) Here are some statistical examples :

(a) For prevalence of younger members in Hitler's Party (from Gerth, p. 530) :

Age composition in percentages of the total population in the years 1931, 1932 and 1935 as compared with the age composition of the Social Democratic Party in 1931 and the total population over 18 years of age in 1933 (excluding Saar, Austria and Sudetenland) :

| Years | National Socialist Party | | | Social Dem. Party | Total Population |
	1931	1932	1935	1931	1933
18-30	37·6	42·2	35·4	19·3	31·1
31-40	27·9	27·8	27·9	27·4	22·0
41-50	19·6	17·1	20·8	26·5	17·1
Over 50	14·9	12·9	15·9	26·8	29·8

Of the 11,160 teachers who worked in honorary jobs in the Hitler Youth on October 1, 1937, those over 40 years of age numbered 15·8 per cent., those between 30 and 40 were 40·5 per cent., and those younger than 30 years were 4·27 per cent. (*Frankfurter Zeitung*, August 3, 1938).

(b) Occupational Distribution of Nazi Party Membership, 1933 and 1935 (after Gerth, p. 527) :

Occupational Classification	Party Membership		Total Gainfully Employed *	
	1933	1935	1933	1933
	(1)	(2)	(3)	(4)
Manual workers . .	31·5	32·1	46·3	38·5
White-collar employees .	21·1	20·6	12·5	12·5
Independents † . .	17·6	20·2	9·6	9·6
Officials . . .	6·7	13·0	4·6	4·6
Peasants . . .	12·6	10·7	21·1	28·9
Others ‡ . . .	10·5	3·4	5·9	5·9

* In column 4 the agricultural wage-workers who were included with " manual workers " in column 3 are classified with " peasants," leaving as manual workers only those employed in non-agricultural pursuits and therefore predominantly urban.

† Skilled artisans, professional persons, merchants, etc., excluding independent peasants.

‡ Domestic servants and non-agricultural family helpers.

The second and third groups, which are heavily over-represented in the Party membership as over the part played by them in the numbers of total gainfully employed, would be those who suffered most from the permanent come-down in the social scale caused by the inflation. Although group I, manual workers, the urban proletariat, and group V, the peasants, suffered equally heavily from the economic depression, they had not transformed this fact into social resentment, and their outsider position was a psychologically different one.

[5] Meanwhile the Atlantic Charter has been published, and there is a greater readiness to discuss problems of Reconstruction on the level of general abstractions or in terms of concrete machinery. It is still true that dynamic ideas, the creative vision, are lacking. These alone really integrate a community and sponsor common action.

[6] Since this has been written, a National Youth Service has been established in Britain. It is to be seen how it will work.

[7] See the description of life in a Nazi Girls' Labour Camp, in Hartshorne, *op. cit.*, pp. 20 ff.

Some more Readings on the Subject

Klaus Mehnert, *Youth in Soviet Russia* (transl. by M. Davidsohn : London, 1933).

H. Spaull, *The Youth of Russia* (London, 1933).

G. F. Kneller, *The Educational Philosophy of National Socialism*, published for the Department of Education in Yale University (Yale and London, 1941) (with extensive bibliography).

A. Thorburn, " Psychological and Other Aspects of Recent Trends in German Education," in *British Journal of Educational Psychology*, vols. v.-vi., 1934-36.

Betty and Ernest K. Lindley, *The New Deal for Youth* (New York, 1939).

" Youth Education To-day," in *Sixteenth Yearbook of the American Association of School Administrators*, National Association (Washington, 1938).

American Youth Commission, *A Program of Action for American Youth* (Washington, 1939).

R. Schairer, " What English War Education teaches the World," in *The Journal of Education and Sociology* (New York, October 1941).

NOTES TO CHAPTER IV

[1] To supplement what has been said in the text I mention some of my other publications on the function and shape of sociology :

K. Mannheim, *Die Gegenwartsaufgaben der Soziologie* (The Task of Sociology in the Present Situation). Opening lecture at a conference of German University teachers of Sociology, held in Frankfurt a. M. in February 1932 (published in German only : Tubingen, 1932).

——, " The Place of Sociology," in *The Social Sciences : Their Relations in Theory and in Teaching* (London : Le Play House Press, 1936).

——, " Adult Education and the Social Sciences," in *Tutors' Bulletin of Adult Education*, Second Series, No. 20 (February 1938).

——, " German Sociology, 1918-33," in *Politica* (February 1934).

Cf. also M. Ginsberg, " The Place of Sociology " ; A. M. Carr-Saunders, " The Place of Sociology " ; T. H. Marshall, " Report on the Teaching of the Social Sciences," in *The Social Sciences : Their Relations in Theory and in Teaching* (London : Le Play House Press, 35 Gordon Square, 1936).

C. A. Beard, " A Charter for the Social Sciences (Report of the Commission on the Social Studies)," in *American Historical Association* (New York, 1932) ; L. C. Marshall and R. M. Goetz, " Curriculum-Making in the Social Studies—A Social Process Approach (Report of the Commission on the Social Studies)," in *American Historical Association*, Part XIII (New York, 1936) ; E. Horn, " Methods of Instruction in the Social Studies (Report of the Commission on the Social Studies)," in *American Historical Association*, Part XV (New York, 1937) ; and the excellent volume, *The Social Studies in General Education*, Report of the Committee on the Function of the Social Studies in General Education for the Commission of Secondary School Curriculum (New York and London, 1938) ; Frederick William Roman, *La Place de la Sociologie dans l'Education aux Etats-Unis* (Paris, 1923) ; A. Walther, *Soziologie und Sozialwissenschaften in Amerika* (Karlsruhe, 1927) ; F. B. Karpf, *American Social Psychology : Its Origins, Development and European Background* (New York, 1932).

Some more Readings on the Subject

A. Flexner, *Universities, American, English, German* (Oxford, 1930).
R. M. Hutchins, *The Higher Learning in America* (New Haven).
N. Foerster, *The American State University*.
A. M. Carr-Saunders, " The Function of Universities in the Modern World," in *Sociological Review*, vol. 32, 1940.
A. Lowe, *The Universities in Transformation* (London, 1940).
F. Clarke, *Essays in the Politics of Education* (London, 1923).
——, *Education and Social Change : An English Interpretation* (London, 1940).
——, " The Social Function of Secondary Education," in *Sociological Review*, 1941.
Sir Richard Livingstone, *The Future in Education* (Cambridge, 1941).
——, *Education for a World Adrift* (Cambridge, 1943).
A. G. Stead, *The Education of a Community—to-day and to-morrow* (London, 1942).
H. C. Dent, *A New Order in English Education* (London, 1942).
H. M. Burton, *The Education of the Countryman*, International Library of Sociology and Social Reconstruction (London, 1943).
M. Reeves and J. Drewett, *What is Christian Education ?* (London, 1942).
F. H. Knight, " Theology and Education," in *American Journal of Sociology*, 1938.
M. W. Kotschnig, *Unemployment in the Learned Professions* (Oxford, 1937).
John Dewey, *School and Society* (Chicago, 1910).
——, *Democracy and Education* (New York, 1914).
W. H. Kilpatrick, *Education for a Changing Civilization* (New York, 1931).
I. L. Kandel, *Competing Theories of Education* (New York, 1938).
C. A. Beard, *The Unique Function of Education in American Democracy*, prepared for the Educational Policies Commission of the National Education Association, 1937.

J. V. Nef, *United States and the Future of Civilization.*
J. H. Newlon, *Education for Democracy in Our Time* (New York, 1940).
R. Ulich, *Fundamentals of Democratic Education* (New York, 1940).
A. N. Whitehead, *The Aims of Education and other Essays* (New York, 1929).

NOTES TO CHAPTER V

[1] Cf. also my " The Sociology of Human Valuations : The Psychological and Sociological Approach," in *Further Papers on the Social Sciences : Their Relations in Theory and in Teaching,* edited by J. E. Dugdale (London : Le Play House Press, 35 Gordon Square, 1935).

[2] I am deliberately giving an elastic definition of adjustment, which leaves scope for a more subtle analysis of the meaning of the word. Adjustment does not necessarily mean mechanical adjustment in which only one response is possible to a given stimulus. Indeed, the opposite seems to be true. Every real human adjustment to social conditions is " creative adjustment " where the " total organism " is related to the " total environment." Creative adjustment is therefore a continuous liberation of new energies, a permanent give-and-take between the original conditions and the human being ; it is progressive experience. Cf. more on the subject, M. P. Follett, *Creative Experience* (London and New York, 1924).

[3] W. I. Thomas and F. Znaniecky, *The Polish Peasant in Europe and America* (New York, 1927), 2 vols., especially pp. 87-106.

[4] Jessie Taft, *The Dynamics of Therapy in a Controlled Relationship,* ch. ii, " Thirty-one Contacts with a Seven-Year-Old Boy " (New York, 1933). Cf. also J. Dollard, *Criteria for the Life History* (published for the Institute of Human Relations by Yale University Press, New Haven, 1935) ; cf. especially pp. 76 f.

[5] Karen Horney, *The Neurotic Personality of our Time* (London, 1937).

[6] M. W. Wulff, " Widerstand des Ich-Ideals und Realitätsanpassung," in *Internationale Zeitschrift für Psychoanalyse,* vol. 12, 1926.

[7] The investigation of these norms which satisfy the needs of the unconscious mind is so much in its beginnings that it is impossible to state either positive or negative rules and correlations. But the acknowledgment of the existence of the needs of the unconscious is to be stressed in order to avoid a pretentious attitude which thinks itself capable of interfering with everything. There is surely something between a blind traditionalism to which everything old is sacrosanct even if its evil consequences are already quite obvious, and that kind of utilitarianism which regards the task of the social philosopher as a kind of human engineering, based on a very narrow-minded conception of efficiency. In contrast to this there is a form of rationality which does not shrink from the use of the mind, but links it up with a sense of creative evolution. It is continuously aware of forces and impulses which have so far been unnoticed, and emerge only in connection with dynamic change. The discussion of these norms which satisfy unconscious needs is taken up once more later on ; cf. pp. 131 seqq., 134, 135-139, 142.

[8] R. G. Foster, " Sociological Research in Adolescence," in *American Journal of Sociology,* 1936.

[9] Louis Wender, " The Dynamics of Group Psycho-therapy and its Application " (read before the New York Neurological Society, April 2, 1935), in *The Journal of Nervous and Mental Disease,* vol. 84, July-December 1936.

[10] F. M. Thrasher, *The Gang : A Study of 1313 Gangs in Chicago,* 2nd ed. (Chicago, 1936) ; J. A. Puffer, *The Boy and his Gang* (Boston, 1912).

[11] A. Aichhorn, " Die Übertragung," in *Zeitschrift für psychoanalytische Pädagogik,* vol. 10, 1936. Cf. also his *Wayward Youth* (New York, 1935, German edition, 1925) ; E. Heath, *The Approach to the Parent* (New York, 1933) ; K. Moore, " A Specialized Method in the Treatment of Parents in a Child Guidance Clinic," in *Psychoanalytic Review,* vol. 21.

[12] More on the problem in my *Ideology and Utopia : An Introduction to the Sociology of Knowledge,* 2nd ed. (London and New York, 1939). Cf. also A. W. Kornhauser, " Analysis of ' Class ' Structure of Contemporary American Society—Psychological

Bases of Class Divisions," in G. W. Hartmann and T. Newcomb (editors), *Industrial Conflict : A Psychological Interpretation* (New York, 1939).
[13] In his study, to be quoted later.
[14] As to the ideologies concerning success in life, cf. also G. Ichheiser, *Die Kritik des Erfolges* (Leipzig, 1930).
[15] P. Schilder, " The Analysis of Ideologies as a Psycho-therapeutic Method especially in Group Treatment," in *American Journal of Psychiatry*, vol. 93, no. 3, November 1936. In the above characteristics of the aims and methods of Wender and Schilder I followed their discussion and concentrated upon those points with which I felt myself in agreement. That means that the stress was laid upon the mechanisms which are accessible to the psycho-analytic approach. Apart from them, ideologies and utopias have their roots in group interests and needs which are closely related to the pressure under which these groups live. The removal of these ideologies or utopias is thus not only a matter of psychological analysis but a question of changing the social and economic position. Nevertheless, neither the purely psychological nor the purely economic and social readjustment is effective in isolation. An important recent analysis is E. Fromm, *The Fear of Freedom*, The International Library of Sociology and Social Reconstruction (London, 1942).
[16] J. Ortega y Gasset, *The Revolt of the Masses* (London, 1932) ; E. Lederer, *State of the Masses* (New York, 1940).
[17] A fairly complete account and a valuable bibliography of these experiments can be found in the article by J. F. Dashiell, " Experimental Studies of the Influence of Social Situations on the Behaviour of Human Adults," in C. Murchison, *A Handbook of Social Psychology*, part vi. (Worcester, Mass., 1935).
[18] Cf. W. O. Döring, *Psychologie der Schulklasse : Eine empirische Untersuchung* (A. W. Zuckfeldt Verlag, 1927) ; A. Kruckenberg, " Die Schulklasse als Lebensform," in *Zeitschrift für pädag. Psychologie und experimentelle Pädagogik*, vol. 25, 1924 ; A. Kruckenberg, *Die Schulklasse* (Leipzig, 1926) ; N. M. Campbell, *The Elementary School Teacher's Treatment of Classroom Problems* (Bureau of Publications, Teachers College, Columbia University, New York, 1935) ; E. Hanfmann, " Social Structure of a Group of Kindergarten Children, *American Journal of Ortopsychiatry*, 1935, 5, 407-410.
[19] H. Gaudig, " Freie geistige Schularbeit in Theorie und Praxis," *Im Auftrag der Zentralstelle für Erziehung und Unterricht* (Berlin, 1922) ; O. Scheibner, " Der Arbeitsvorgang in technischer, psychologischer und pädagogischer Verfassung," in the same volume. As to the problem of " occupational therapy " and its application in this country, cf. Government publications, United Kingdom, *Memorandum on Occupational Therapy for Mental Patients* (1933). Cf. also A. Meyer, *Philosophy of Occupational Therapy*, vol. i. (1924).
[20] Cf. M. Y. Reaney, *The Psychology of the Organized Group Game, with Special Reference to its Place in the Play-System and its Educational Value*. Thesis. London. The British Journal of Psychology Monograph Supplements, No. 4, 1916. (Good bibliography.) H. C. Lehman and P. A. Witty, " *The Psychology of Play Activities* (New York, 1927) ; E. Liss, " Play Techniques in Child Analysis," in *American Journal of Ortopsychiatry*, vol. 6, January 1936 ; S. H. Britt and S. Q. Janus, " Towards a Social Psychology of Play," *Journal of Social Psychology*, 1941.
[21] Cf. Reaney, *op. cit.*
[22] F. H. Allport, *Institutional Behaviour* (Chapel Hill, 1933).
[23] Cf. F. C. Bartlett, " Group Organization and Social Behaviour," in *International Journal of Ethics*, vol. 35, 1924-25 ; R. E. Park, " Human Nature and Collective Behaviour," in *American Journal of Sociology*, vol. 32 ; G. L. Coyle, *Social Process in Organized Groups*, in Contemporary Society Series, ed. by MacIver (good bibliography) ; C. R. Rogers, " The Intelligent Use of Clubs, Groups, and Camps," in his *The Clinical Treatment of the Problem Child* (Boston, New York, etc., 1939) (good bibliography) ; E. B. South, " Some Psychological Aspects of Committee Work," in *Journal of Applied Psychology*, 1927, vol. ii. 348-368, 437-464 ; H. L. Hollingworth, *The Psychology of the Audience* (New York, 1935) ; W. R. Smith, " Social Education in School through Group Activities," in *Publications of the American Sociological Society*, vol. 13, 1918 ; S. R. Slavson, *Creative Group Education* (New York, 1937) ; W. H. Kilpatrick, *Group Education for a Democracy* (New York, 1941).
[24] B. Bosch, " Massenführer, Gruppenführer," in *Zeitschrift für pädagogische*

Psychologie, vol. 30 (6), 1929 ; H. W. Busch, *Leadership or Group Work*, chap. v., "Types of Group-Leadership" (New York, 1934) ; E. De A. Partridge, *Leadership among Adolescent Boys* (New York, 1934).

NOTES TO CHAPTER VI

[1] War provides fields of experience for the study of the effects of group integration and disintegration upon the mind. A carefully organized teamwork for the observation of changes as they develop under our eyes would yield most valuable results. A stimulating symposium on this topic was held in the Medical Section of the British Psychological Society—Speakers : C. Baines, E. Glover, K. Mannheim. See my "Changes in our Psychic Economy Caused by the War," in *Internationale Zeitschrift für Psychoanalyse und Imago*, vol. 25, London, 1940 (in German). Cf. also *German Psychological Warfare, Survey and Bibliography*, ed. by L. Farago and L. F. Grittler, published by the New York Committee for National Morale, 1941, and the issues on "Morale" of *The American Journal of Sociology*, vol. xlvii, No. 3, Nov. 1941, and of *The Journal of Educational Sociology*, vol. 15, no. 7, 1942, March.

NOTES TO CHAPTER VII

[1] Cf. Chapter II of this book.

[2] Max Weber, *The Protestant Ethic and the Spirit of Capitalism* (transl. by T. Parsons : London, 1930).

[3] Cf. Max Weber, "Politik als Beruf" (reprinted in his *Gesammelte Politische Schriften*, München, 1921, pp. 441 ff.).

[4] In my *Ideology and Utopia : An Introduction to the Sociology of Knowledge* (London and New York, 2nd ed., 1939) I tried to show the axiomatic foundations of different approaches to history and politics. See especially the chapter on "Prospects of Scientific Politics."

[5] Cf. Max Weber, *The Protestant Ethic and the Spirit of Capitalism* (London, 1930).

[6] Alfred Weber, "Prinzipielles zur Kultursoziologie," in *Archiv für Sozialwissenschaft und Sozialpolitik*, vol. 47.

[7] Paradigm : pattern, exemplar, example (Oxford English Dictionary). "Paradigmatic experiences" in our context will mean those decisive, basic experiences which are felt to reveal the meaning of life as a whole. Their pattern is so deeply impressed upon our mind that they provide a mould into which further experiences flow. Thus once formed they lend shape to later experiences.

[8] In this sense adjustment is only lacking if behaviour has no real reference to the situation, if it does not try to solve the conflicts presented by the environment. But exactly this happens if one acts under the spell of orthodoxy according to an established pattern irrespective of the entirely changed situation. Withdrawal reaction, of course, may be a form of adequate adjustment, as long as it is an actual and relevant adjustment based upon what in German is called *Auseinandersetzung*. To paraphrase an apt remark of a modern writer : even the pigeons in Trafalgar Square adjust themselves to the presence of the National Gallery in their environment, but the question is if theirs is a relevant and adequate adjustment to the real purpose of the object.

[9] The implications of this problem are not yet explored. I tried to discuss it on pp. 79-86 of this book.

[10] Jakob Burckhardt spoke of "primordial images," C. G. Jung of "archetypes," thereby using a concept of St. Augustin's (cf. C. G. Jung, *Two Essays on Analytical Psychology* (London, 1928) ; *The Integration of Personality* (London, 1940) ; and his *Psychological Types* (London, 1933)). For our purposes it is not necessary to embark upon the question whether they are inherited through the brain structure from one generation to the next, and whether we have to introduce the hypothesis of a collective unconscious. (Freud acknowledges only the personal unconscious.) For us it is more important to prove their presence in the history of our cultural development,

especially to analyse the social function they fulfil, and to point to the unfilled gap and the disturbances which are caused if they disappear.

¹¹ Cf. pp. 17-18 of this book. Primary groups in Cooley's terminology are the family, the neighbourhood and the village community.

¹² See E. Y. Hartshorne, *German Youth and the Nazi Dream* (New York and Toronto, 1941).

¹³ Cf. pp. 119-120 of this book.

¹⁴ Max Weber, *op. cit.*

¹⁵ Another line of approach is indicated in Chapter V of this book, where the experiments in group analysis are discussed.

¹⁶ See " The Workers' Incentive in a Planned Society," in *Labour Discussion Notes*, no. 26 (London, September 1941). Suggestions of this article have been utilized in the list given. Further contributions to the whole sphere of problems are contained in R. G. Valentine, " The Human Element in Production," in *American Journal of Sociology*, vol. 22, no. 4 ; H. W. Hess, " Human Aspects of Business in the New Consumption Era," in *Annals of the American Academy of Political and Social Science*, vol. 165. Cf. also E. Mayo, *The Human Problems of an Industrial Civilization* (New York, 1933) ; J. N. Whitehead, *Leadership in a Free Society* (Cambridge, Mass., 1936).

¹⁷ Cf. the corresponding chapter in my *Man and Society in an Age of Reconstruction*, pp. 265-327.

¹⁸ J. A. Hobson, *Work and Wealth* (New York and London, 1914).

[INDEX OF SUBJECTS

INDEX OF SUBJECTS

INDEX OF NAMES

The International Library of
SOCIOLOGY AND SOCIAL RECONSTRUCTION
Editor: KARL MANNHEIM
Professor of Education in the University of London

ADVISORY BOARD: HAROLD BUTLER, C.B., Minister in Charge of British Information Services at H.M. Embassy, Washington; Sir ALEXANDER CARR-SAUNDERS, Director of the London School of Economics; SIR FRED CLARKE, M.A. (Oxon) ; LORD LINDSAY, C.B.E., Master of Balliol College, Oxford.

PLAN OF THE LIBRARY
Sections

KEGAN PAUL, TRENCH, TRUBNER & CO. LTD.
68-74 Carter Lane, London, E.C.4

SOCIOLOGY OF EDUCATION

Mission of the University
by ORTEGA Y GASSET. Translated and introduced by HOWARD LEE
NOSTRAND   *7s. 6d.*

Total Education: A Plea for Synthesis
by M. L. JACKS, Director, Department of Education, Oxford University
10s. 6d.

Education in Transition
A Sociological Analysis of the Impact of the War on English Education
by H. C. DENT   *Fourth Impression.   12s. 6d.*

The Reform of Secondary Education
by H. C. DENT   *About 15s.*

The Education of the Countryman
by H. M. BURTON   *Second Impression.   15s.*

Education for Adults: A Study in Transition
by T. MACKAY MURE   *About 10s. 6d.*

Adult Education in a Progressive Democracy
Historical Studies and a Programme for the Future by H. E. POOLE,
Organising Secretary of the W.E.A., Norfolk; PAUL H. SHEATS,
Professor of Education, Pres. of the Dept. of Adult Education of the
Nat. Educ. Assoc., U.S.A.; DAVID CUSHMAN COYLE, U.S.A., Assistant
Director of Town Hall, New York; E. BORINSKI, Dr. Phil.   *About 21s.*

Who Shall Be Educated? The Challenge of Unequal Opportunities
by W. LLOYD WARNER, Prof. of Anthropology and Sociology, Member
of Comm. on Human Development, Univ. of Chicago; ROBERT J.
HAVIGHURST, Prof. of Education, Member of Comm. on Human
Development, Univ. of Chicago; MARTIN B. LOEB, Inst. of Child
Welfare, Univ. of California, at Berkeley   *10s. 6d.*

Natural Science and Education: A Sociological Study
by J. A. LAUWERYS, Reader in Education in the Univ. of London
About 15s.

2

The Social Psychology of Education: A Sociological Study
by C. M. FLEMING, Ed.B., Ph.D., University of London Institute of Education   *Third Impression.*   *7s. 6d.*

German Youth: Bond or Free
by HOWARD BECKER, Professor of Sociology, University of Wisconsin
Illustrated.   *18s.*

The Museum: Its History and Its Tasks in Education
by ALMA S. WITTLIN, Dr. Phil.   *In preparation.   Illustrated.   About 21s.*

SOCIOLOGY OF RELIGION

The Sociology of Religion
by JOACHIM WACH   *About 10s. 6d.*

Religion and the Economic Order
by FRANK KNIGHT, Prof. of Social Sciences, University of Chicago, and THORNTON W. MERRIAM, Director of U.S.O. Training Nat. Council of the Y.M.C.A.   *In preparation.   About 21s.*

SOCIOLOGY OF ART

Sociology of the Renaissance
by ALFRED VON MARTIN, translated by W. L. LUETKENS
Second Impression.   8s. 6d.

SOCIOLOGY OF LANGUAGE AND LITERATURE

The Sociology of Literary Taste
by LEVIN L. SCHÜCKING, Dr. Phil.   *Second Impression.   7s. 6d.*

3

Authors and the Public in Eighteenth-Century England
by ALEXANDRE BELJAME. Edited with an Introduction by Prof.
BONAMY DOBREE. Translated by E. O. LORIMER *About 21s.*

Chekhov and His Russia
by W. H. BRUFORD, M.A., Professor of German in the University of
Edinburgh *About 21s.*

SOCIOLOGICAL APPROACH TO THE STUDY OF HISTORY

**The Aftermath of the Napoleonic Wars: The Concert
of Europe—An Experiment**
by H. G. SCHENK, D.Phil. (Oxon) *Illustrated. 16s.*

**Progress and Disenchantment: A Comparative Study
of European Romanticism**
by H. G. SCHENK, D.Phil. (Oxon) *Illustrated. About 21s.*

SOCIOLOGY OF LAW

The Sociology of Law
by GEORGES GURVITCH, formerly Prof. of Sociology, University of
Strassbourg, France. With an Introduction by ROSCOE POUND, Prof.
of Jurisprudence, late Dean of the Faculty of Law, Harvard University
18s.

**The Institutions of Civil Law and Their Social
Functions**
by KARL RENNER, Chancellor of the Austrian Republic. Edited with an
Introduction by O. KAHN-FREUND, Ll.M., Dr. Jur., Lecturer in Law,
University of London *About 10s. 6d.*

Corporations and Their Control
by A. B. LEVY, Dr. Jur., C.L.S., Cantab. *2 vols. About 18s. each*

The Control of Industrial Combinations
by ANDREW NEUGROSCHEL, Ph.D., Dr. Jur., Dr. Pol., of the Middle
Temple, Barrister-at-Law *About 15s.*

Legal Aid

by ROBERT EGERTON, Hon. Sec. Legal Sub-committee Cambridge House, Solicitor of the Supreme Court. With an Introduction by D. L. GOODHART, K.C., D.C.L., Ll.D., Prof. of Jurisprudence, Oxford   *10s. 6d.*

Soviet Legal Theory: Its Social Background and Development

by RUDOLF SCHLESINGER, Ph.D., London   *16s.*

CRIMINOLOGY AND THE SOCIAL SERVICES

Criminal Justice and Social Reconstruction

by HERMANN MANNHEIM, Dr. Jur., Lecturer in Criminology in the University of London   *15s.*

The Psycho-Analytical Approach to Juvenile Delinquency: Theory, Case Studies, Treatment

by KATE FRIEDLANDER, M.D., L.R.C.P. (Edin.), D.P.M. (Lond.), Hon. Psychiatrist, Inst. for the Scientific Treatment of Delinquency; Clinical Dir., W. Sussex Child Guidance Service   *18s.*

Voluntary Social Services in Britain

by HENRY A. MESS, late Reader in Social Science in the University of London. Edited by GERTRUDE WILLIAMS, Lecturer in Economics, University of London   *About 21s.*

SOCIOLOGY AND POLITICS

The Analysis of Political Behaviour: An Empirical Approach

by HAROLD D. LASSWELL, Formerly Prof. Polit. Science in the University of Chicago, now Director, War Communications Research, Library of Congress   *About 18s.*

Democracy, Political Representation and the Electoral System: An Analysis of Fundamentals

by GERHARD LEIBHOLZ, Dr. Phil.   *About 21s.*

5

Dictatorship and Political Police

The Technique of Control by Fear by E. K. BRAMSTEDT, Ph.D. (London)

15s.

Nationality in History and Politics

by FREDERICK HERTZ, Author of "Race and Civilisation"

Second Impression. 25s.

The American Dilemma

The Negro Problem and Modern Democracy by GUNNAR MYRDAL, Prof. of Political Economy and Public Finance, Stockholm Univ.

2 vols. About £2. 2s.

FOREIGN AFFAIRS, THEIR SOCIAL, POLITICAL AND ECONOMIC FOUNDATIONS

Patterns of Peacemaking

by DAVID THOMSON, Ph.D., Cantab., Research Fellow of Sidney Sussex Coll., Cambridge; E. MEYER, Dr. rer. pol., and A. BRIGGS, B.A., Cantab.

21s.

French Canada in Transition

by EVERETT C. HUGHES, Professor of Sociology, University of Chicago

15s.

State and Economics in the Middle East

by A. BONNE, Dr. œc. publ., Director, Economic Research Institute of Palestine

About 25s.

Economic Development of the Middle East

An Outline of Planned Reconstruction by A. BONNE, Dr. œc. publ., Director, Economic Research Institute of Palestine

Second Impression. 12s. 6d.

Federalism in Central and Eastern Europe

by RUDOLF SCHLESINGER, Ph.D., London

30s.

The Danube Basin and the German Economic Sphere

by ANTONIN BASCH, Dr. Phil., Columbia Univ.

18s.

The Regions of Germany
by R. E. DICKINSON, Reader in Geography, University College, London
Second Impression. *10s. 6d.*

MIGRATION AND RE-SETTLEMENT

Economics of Migration
by JULIUS ISAAC, Ph.D., London. With an Introduction by A. M. CARR-
SAUNDERS, Director of the London School of Economics *18s.*

Co-operative Communities at Work: A Comparative Study
by HENRIK INFIELD, Director, Rural Settlement Inst., New York
About 15s.

ECONOMIC PLANNING

Plan for Reconstruction
by W. H. HUTT, Prof. of Commerce, University of Capetown
Second Impression. *18s.*

Danger Spots in the New Economic Controls
by Dr. F. BURCHARDT and G. D. N. WORSWICK, Institute of
Statistics, University of Oxford *About 15s.*

Retail Trade Associations
A New Form of Monopolist Organisation in Britain, by HERMANN
LEVY, Author of "The New Industrial System" *Second Impression.* *15s.*

The Shops of Britain: A Study in Retail Trade Distribution
by HERMANN LEVY *About 21s.*

The Price of Social Security—The Problem of Labour Mobility
by GERTRUDE WILLIAMS, Lecturer in Economics, University of London
Second Impression. *12s. 6d.*

7

SOCIOLOGY OF THE FAMILY AND ALLIED TOPICS

Nation and Family

The Swedish Experiment in Democratic Family and Population Policy
by ALVA MYRDAL   *21s.*

The Sociology of Women's Work

by GERTRUDE WILLIAMS, Lecturer in Economics, University of London
About 15s.

The Adolescent: A Psychological Sociological Approach

by C. M. FLEMING, Ed.B., Ph.D., University of London Institute of
Education   *About 15s.*

TOWN AND COUNTRY PLANNING. HUMAN ECOLOGY

Creative Demobilisation

Vol. I. Principles of National Planning
By E. A. GUTKIND, D.Ing.

Vol. 2. Case Studies in National Planning
Edited by E. A. GUTKIND, D.Ing.   *Second Impression. 21s. each*

Revolution of Environment

by E. A. GUTKIND, D.Ing.   *Illustrated. 30s.*

The Journey to Work

by K. LIEPMANN, Ph.D., London. With an Introduction by A. M.
Carr-Saunders, Director of the London School of Economics
Second Impression. 15s.

City, Region and Regionalism

by ROBERT E. DICKINSON, Reader in Geography, University College,
London. With Maps and Plans   *About 25s.*

SOCIOLOGICAL STUDIES OF MODERN COMMUNITIES

Negroes in Britain

The Anthropology of some Coloured Communities in Great Britain
with Comparative Material on Colour Prejudice
by E. K. LITTLE, Ph.D., London   *About 15s.*

8

Co-operative Living in Palestine
by HENRIK F. INFIELD, Director, Rural Settlement Inst., New York
In preparation. Illustrated. 7s. 6d.

ANTHROPOLOGY AND COLONIAL POLICY

Malay Fishermen: Their Peasant Economy
by RAYMOND FIRTH, Prof. of Anthropology, University of London
Illustrated. 25s. net

The Malay Peasant
An Economic Survey of Past Conditions and Future Problems by
RAYMOND FIRTH, Prof. of Anthropology, University of London
About 21s.

Peasant Life in China
by HSIAO T'UNG FEI, Ph.D., London *Third Impression. Illustrated. 15s.*

Hsinlung Hsiang
A Field Study of Peasant Life in the Red Basin, West China
by ISABEL CROOK and YU HSI-CHI *About 21s.*

A Japanese Village: Suye Mura
by JOHN P. EMBREE, Visiting Assoc. Prof. of Anthropology, University
of Chicago. With an Introduction by A. R. RADCLIFFE-BROWN,
Professor of Social Anthropology, Oxford University
Illustrated. 18s.

The Golden Wing: A Family Chronicle
by LIN HUEH-HWA, with an Introduction by BRUNO LASKER,
Internat. Secretariat, Inst. of Pacific Relations *About 15s.*

SOCIOLOGY AND PSYCHOLOGY OF THE
PRESENT CRISIS

Diagnosis of Our Time
by KARL MANNHEIM, Lecturer in Sociology, University of London
Third Impression. 10s. 6d.

Farewell to European History—Beyond Nihilism
by ALFRED WEBER *About 30s.*

The Fear of Freedom
by Dr. ERICH FROMM   *Third Impression. 15s.*

Human Nature and Enduring Peace
Edited by GARDNER MURPHY, Professor, The College of the City of
New York   *About 15s.*

The Autonomy of Science
by MICHAEL POLANYI, F.R.S., Prof. of Chemistry, University of
Manchester   *About 15s.*

SOCIAL PSYCHOLOGY AND
PSYCHO-ANALYSIS

Psychology and the Social Pattern
by JULIAN BLACKBURN, Ph.D., B.Sc. (Econ.), Lecturer on Social
Psychology, London School of Economics   *Second Impression. 10s. 6d.*

The Framework of Human Behaviour
by JULIAN BLACKBURN, Ph.D., B.Sc. (Econ.), Lecturer on Social
Psychology, London School of Economics   *About 10s. 6d.*

Individual Development in Society
by JULIAN BLACKBURN, Ph.D., B.Sc. (Econ.), Lecturer on Social
Psychology, London School of Economics   *About 10s. 6d.*
(Three independent volumes supplementing each other)

A Handbook of Social Psychology
by KIMBALL YOUNG, Professor of Sociology, Queens College, New
York   *21s.*

Freud—An Introduction
Selected Readings and a Study concerning the Relationship between
Psycho-analysis and Sociology by WALTER HOLLITSCHER, Dr. Phil.
                                             About 15s.

Social Learning and Imitation
by NEAL E. MILLER and JOHN DOLLARD of the Institute of Human
Relations, Yale University   *15s.*

Frustration and Aggression
by JOHN DOLLARD, LEONARD E. DOOB, NEAL E. MILLER, O. H.
MOWRER, ROBERT R. SEARS, etc., of the Institute of Human
Relations, Yale University   *10s. 6d.*

APPROACHES TO THE PROBLEM
OF PERSONALITY

The Cultural Background of Personality
by RALPH LINTON, Professor of Anthropology, Columbia University
About 12s. 6d.

The Feminine Character. The History of an Ideology
by VIOLA KLEIN, Ph.D., London. With an Introduction by KARL MANNHEIM, Dr. Phil., Lecturer in Sociology, University of London
12s. 6d.

The History of Autobiography in Antiquity
by GEORG MISCH. Translated by E. W. DICKES   *About 21s.*

PHILOSOPHICAL AND SOCIAL FOUNDATIONS
OF THOUGHT

The Political Element in Economic Theory
by GUNNAR MYRDAL, Professor of Political Economy and Public Finance, University of Stockholm   *About 21s.*

The Ideal Foundations of Economic Thought
by W. STARK, Dr. rer. pol., Dr. Jur.   *Second Impression. 15s.*

The History of Economics in Its Relation to Social Development
by W. STARK, Dr. rer. pol., Dr. Jur.   *Second Impression. 7s. 6d.*

The Decline of Liberalism as an Ideology
by J. H. HALLOWELL   *12s. 6d.*

Society and Nature: A Sociological Inquiry
by HANS KELSEN, Formerly Prof. of Law, Vienna and Geneva, Department of Political Science, University of California   *21s.*

GENERAL SOCIOLOGY

A Handbook of Sociology
by W. F. OGBURN, Professor of Sociology, University of Chicago, and M. F. NIMKOFF, Professor of Sociology, Bucknell University
About 30s.

FOREIGN CLASSICS OF SOCIOLOGY

Wilhelm Dilthey: Selected Readings from his Works and an Introduction to his Sociological and Philosophical Work

by H. A. HODGES, Prof. of Philosophy, University of Reading *10s. 6d.*

George Herbert Mead: An Introduction

Selected Readings from his Works with an Introduction to his Sociological and Philosophical Writings by Dr. MILTON B. SINGER, University of Chicago *About 21s.*

From Max Weber: Essays in Sociology

Translated, edited, and with an Introduction by H. H. GERTH and C. W. MILLS *About 21s.*

DOCUMENTARY

Peace Aims of the United Nations

Documents and Readings. Edited by DAVID THOMSON, Ph.D., Cantab, Research Fellow of Sidney Sussex College, Cambridge, and E. MEYER, Dr. rer. pol. *About 21s.*

Changing Attitudes in Soviet Russia

Documents and Readings concerning the *Family*
Edited by R. SCHLESINGER, Ph.D., London *About 21s.*

Changing Attitudes in Soviet Russia

Documents and Readings concerning *National Autonomy and Experiments in Administrative Devolution*
Edited by R. SCHLESINGER, Ph.D., London *About 21s.*

Changing Attitudes in Soviet Russia

Documents and Readings concerning *Foreign Policy*
Edited by R. SCHLESINGER, Ph.D., London *About 21s.*

All prices are net

Publishers in the United States of America
OXFORD UNIVERSITY PRESS, NEW YORK

THE WESTMINSTER PRESS, LONDON, W.9